C++14 F

Chandra Shekhar Kumar

T_EX is a trademark of the American Mathematical Society.
METAFONT is a trademark of Addison-Wesley.

For comments, suggestions and or feedback, send mail to :
chandrashekhar.kumar@gmail.com

For permission, send mail to : *chandrashekhar.kumar@gmail.com*

ISBN-13: 978-1500239879
ISBN-10: 1500239879

Preface

This book contains selected questions related to C++14 with detailed solutions to all of these which will help the reader to hone her skills to solve a particular problem.

Primary sources of this collection are:

1. *Advanced C++ FAQs: Volume 1 : Fundamentals*
2. *Advanced C++ FAQs: Volume 2 : Generic Programming*
3. *Advanced C++ FAQs: Volumes 1 & 2*

This book is not an introduction to C++. It assumes that the reader is aware of the basics of C++98 and C++03 and wants to expand her horizon to latest and greatest in C++14(aka C++1y). The problems are marked on a scale of one(*)(simplest) to five stars(*****)(hardest).

Forthcoming volumes will strengthen this particular approach spanning various areas of C++.

For suggestions, feedback and comments, please contact :
chandrashekhar.kumar@gmail.com

Chandra Shekhar Kumar

List of Chapters

List of Chapters

0.1 variable templates

*** Question 1   variable template

What is a *variable template* ?

Solution of Question 1

A *variable template* is a declaration which is introduced by a template declaration of a variable. As we already know that a template declaration is also a definition if its declaration defines a function, a class, a variable, or a static data member.

A *variable template* at class scope is a *static data member template.*

Consider a simple template meta function, which uses variable template feature to store the boolean value of result of comparing two types:

```
template <typename T, typename U>
constexpr bool is_same = std::is_same<T, U>::value;

bool t = is_same<int, int>; // true
bool f = is_same<int, float>; // false
```

The types of variable templates are not restricted to just built-in types; they can be user defined types.

```
struct matrix_constants
{
    template<typename T>
    using pauli = hermitian_matrix<T, 2>;

    template<typename T>
    constexpr pauli<T> sigma1 = { { 0, 1 }, { 1, 0 } };

    template<typename T>
    constexpr pauli<T> sigma2 = { { 0, -1i }, { 1i, 0 } };

    template<typename T>
    constexpr pauli<T> sigma3 = { { 1, 0 }, { -1, 0 } };
};
```

It makes definitions and uses of parameterized constants much simpler, leading to simplified and more uniform programming rules to teach and to remember like:

```
template<typename T>
struct lexical_cast_fn
{
    template<typename U>
    T operator()(U const &u) const
    {
        //...
    }
};

template<typename T>
constexpr lexical_cast_fn<T> lexical_cast{};

int main()
{
    lexical_cast<int>("42");
}
```

0.2 Constexpr static data members of class templates

*** Question 2   Constexpr static data members of class templates

What is issue with constexpr static data members of class templates ?

Solution of Question 2

Let us revisit how *std::is_same* is designed:

```
 1 template<typename T, T v>
 2 struct integral_constant
 3 {
 4     static constexpr T value = v;
 5     typedef T value_type;
 6     ....
 7 };
 8
 9 template<typename T, T v>
10 constexpr T integral_constant<T, v>::value;
11
12 typedef integral_constant<bool, true>  true_type;
13 typedef integral_constant<bool, false> false_type;
14
15 template<typename T, typename U>
16 struct is_same : false_type{};
17
18 template<typename T>
19 struct is_same<T, T> : true_type{};
```

The main problems with *static data member* are:

- they require *duplicate* declarations:
    1. once inside the class template,
    2. once outside the class template to provide the real definition in case the constants is odr(One Definition Rule) used.
- It creates confusion by the necessity of providing twice the same declaration, whereas ordinary constant declarations do not need duplicate declarations.

The standard class *numeric_limits* also suffers from the same problem as far as constexpr static data members are concerned.

0.3   constexpr function templates

*** Question 3   constexpr function templates

What is issue with constexpr function templates ?

Solution of Question 3

Constexpr functions templates provide functional abstraction.

A simple constexpr function template :

```
 1 template <typename T, typename U>
 2 constexpr bool is_same()
 3 {
 4     return std::is_same<T, U>::value;
 5 }
```

Constexpr functions templates do not have the duplicate declarations issue that static data members have.

However, they force us to chose in advance, at the definition site, how the constants are to be delivered: either by a const reference, or by plain non-reference type.

If delivered by const reference then the constants must be systematically be allocated in static storage.

If by non-reference type, then the constants need copying.

Copying isn't an issue for built-in types, but it is an issue for user-defined types with value semantics that aren't just wrappers around tiny built-in types

Whereas ordinary const(expr) variables do not suffer from this problem. A simple definition is provided, and the decision of whether the constants actually needs to be layout out in storage only depends on the usage, not the definition.

Another examples are the static member functions of *std::numeric_limits* and functions like *boost :: constants :: pi < T > ()*:

```
 1 #include <boost/math/constants/constants.hpp>
 2
 3 template <class Real>
 4 Real area(Real r)
```

```
5 {
6     using namespace boost::math::constants;
7     return pi<Real>() * r * r;
8 }
```

The function template versions of the constants are simple inline functions that return a constant of the correct precision for the type used. In addition, these functions are declared constexpr for those compilers that support this, allowing the result to be used in constant expressions provided the template argument is a literal type.

It looks like we are creating constexpr functions only to return a constant.

0.4   variable templates in action

** Question 4   variable templates in action

Illustrate how *variable templates* can be used to compute the area of a circle for a given type with appropriate precision?

Solution of Question 4

variable templates address both of the issues illustrated before and no syntax modification was required to incorporate this feature in C++11 because current grammar allows any declaration to be parameterized. It was prohibited earlier via semantic constraints which is relaxed now on template declarations.

Let us first represent the mathematical constant π with precision dictated by a floating point datatype:

Program 1: π and variable template

```
1 #include <iostream>
2 #include <iomanip>
3
4 template<typename T>
5 constexpr T pi = T(3.1415926535897932385);
6
7 int main()
8 {
9     std::cout << std::setprecision(40);
10    std::cout << "pi<int> : " << pi<int> << std::endl;
11    std::cout << "pi<float> : " << pi<float> << std::endl;
12    std::cout << "pi<double> : " << pi<double> << std::endl;
13 }
```

With the following command:

```
clang++ -std=c++1y variable_template.cpp
```

we get the following output:

```
pi<int> : 3
pi<float> : 3.14159274101257324218750
pi<double> : 3.141592653589793115997963468544185161591
```

This variable template can be used in a generic function to compute the area of a circle for a given radius:

```
1 template<typename T>
2 T area_circle(T r)
3 {
4     return pi<T> * r * r;
5 }
```

0.5 static data member template

** Question 5   static data member template

Provide a suitable definition of the static data member template *min*:

```
1 struct limits
2 {
3     template<typename T>
4     static const T min; // declaration of min
5 };
```

Solution of Question 5

As we already know that a variable template at class scope is a *static data member template* and a definition for a static data member or static data member template may be provided in a namespace scope enclosing the definition of the static member's class template.

```
1 struct limits
2 {
3     template<typename T>
4     static const T min; // declaration of min
5 };
6
7 template<typename T>
8 const T limits::min = { }; // definition of min
```

0.6 specialization of variable template

*** Question 6   specialization of variable template

Simplify the program below to do the needful:

```
1 template <typename T, typename U>
2 constexpr bool is_same = std::is_same<T, U>::value;
3
4 bool t = is_same<int, int>; // true
5 bool f = is_same<int, float>; // false
```

Solution of Question 6

Variable templates are subject to template specialization like template functions, so we can simplify the code as follows:

```
1 template<typename T, typename U>
2 constexpr bool is_same = false;
3
4 template<typename T>
5 constexpr bool is_same<T, T> = true;
```

0.7 default argument and specialization of variable template

*** Question 7   default argument and specialization of variable template

What is the output of the program ?

```
1 #include <iostream>
2 #include <iomanip>
3
4 template<typename T=double>
5 constexpr T pi = T(3.1415926535897932385);
6
7 template<>
8 constexpr float pi<int> = pi<float>;
9
10 int main()
```

```
11 {
12     std::cout << std::setprecision(30);
13     std::cout << "pi<> : " << pi<> << std::endl;
14     std::cout << "pi<int> : " << pi<int> << std::endl;
15     std::cout << "pi<float> : " << pi<float> << std::endl;
16 }
```

Solution of Question 7

```
pi<> : 3.14159265358979311599796346854
pi<int> : 3.1415927410125732421875
pi<float> : 3.1415927410125732421875
```

0.8 lambda and variable template

*** Question 8   lambda and variable template

Simplify the program below.

```
1 template<typename T>
2 T area_circle(T r)
3 {
4     return pi<T> * r * r;
5 }
```

Solution of Question 8

```
1 template<typename T>
2 auto area_circle = [](auto r) { return pi<T> * r * r; };
```

0.9 variable templates variables vary

** Question 9   variable templates variables vary

Is this a legal code ?

```
1 #include <iostream>
2
3 template<typename T>
4 T magicVal = 42;
5
6 int main()
7 {
8     std::cout << magicVal<int> << std::endl;;
9
10     magicVal<int> = 0;
11
12     std::cout << magicVal<int> << std::endl;;
13 }
```

If yes, what is the output ?

Solution of Question 9

Yes, the code is correct because variable template instances are first-class objects.
Output is :

```
42
0
```

0.10 auto variable templates

** Question 10   variable templates variables vary

Is this a legal code ?

```
1 template<class> constexpr auto X = 42;
2
3 int main()
4 {
5         static_assert(X<int> == 42, "");
6 }
```

Solution of Question 10

Yes, a specialization of a variable template is a variable and as per the standard : *No diagnostic shall be issued for a template for which a valid specialization can be generated.*

0.11 valid specialization but error ?

*** Question 11   valid specialization but error

Why this code doesn't compile ?

```
1 class Y
2 {
3     typedef int type;
4 };
5
6 template<Y::type N>
7 struct X { };
```

Solution of Question 11

Typical error is:

```
specialize.cpp:3:17: error: 'typedef int Y::type' is private
    typedef int type;
                ^
specialize.cpp:6:13: error: within this context
  template<Y::type N>
             ^
```

Because the template parameter declaration is ill-formed, it gets diagnosed immediately and does not form any larger structure. Hence there is no template to be specialized in the first place. There is no "being ill-formed", because ill-formedness implies the state of not being.

So, if the parameter is nonsensical, then we don't have a template declaration. And if the template declaration itself is nonsensical, we don't have a declaration to specialize, hencde the compiler error is issued.

0.12 variable templates and lambda revisited

*** Question 12   variable templates and lambda revisited

Exploit *variable templates* and *lambda* to compute the area of a circle class.

Solution of Question 12

```
1 template<typename T>
2 struct Circle
3 {
4     T radius;
5
6     using value_type = T;
7
```

```
 8       Circle(T r) : radius(r) {}
 9       Circle(const Circle& c) : radius(c.radius) {}
10 };
11
12 template<typename T=double>
13 constexpr T pi = T(3.1415926535897932385);
14
15 auto area = [](auto c )
16 {
17     using T = typename decltype(c)::value_type;
18     return pi<T> * c.radius * c.radius;
19 };
```

Alternatively:

```
1 template<typename T>
2 using f_type = T(*)(Circle<T>);
3
4 template<typename T>
5 f_type<T> area = [](Circle<T> c )
6 {
7     return pi<T> * c.radius * c.radius;
8 };
```

0.13 Incremental improvement to integral_constant

*** Question 13   Incremental improvement to integral_constant

Revisit the class template *is_arithmetic*:

```
1 template <class T>
2 struct is_arithmetic
3       :
4       integral_constant<
5       bool,
6       is_integral<T>::value ||
7       is_floating_point<T>::value
8 > {};
```

Before C++14, the typical usage of such a class template was:

```
1 std::is_arithmetic<T>::value
```

or

```
1 static_cast<bool>(std::is_arithmetic<T>{})
```

What was the increment improvement to the class *integral_constant* to enable simplified usage like

```
1 std::is_arithmetic<T>{}()
```

Solution of Question 13

The following addition was made in order to allow the template to serve as a source of compile-time function objects:

```
1 constexpr value_type operator()() { return value; }
```

So the final class looked like:

```
1 template <class T, T v>
2 struct integral_constant
3 {
4     static constexpr T value = v;
5     using value_type = T;
6     using type = integral_constant<T,v>;
7
8     constexpr operator value_type() { return value; }
9
10    constexpr value_type operator()() { return value; } // C++14
11 };
```

0.14   is_same musings

** Question 14   is_same musing

Enumerate different ways to use *is_same* < *T,U* >.

Solution of Question 14

1. As a function object:

   std :: is_same<T, U>()

2. As a compile time evaluation by invoking the nested *value_type*:

   std :: is_same<T, U>:: value

3. By having a template alias as follows:

   template<typename T, **typename** U>
   using is_same_v = **typename std** :: is_same<T, U>:: value ;

   Now we can use it like

   is_same_v<T, U>()

4. In C++11:

   static__cast<bool>(**std** :: is_same<T, U>{})

5. Using variable template like:

   template<typename T, **typename** U>
   constexpr **bool** is_same = **false** ;

   template<typename T>
   constexpr **bool** is_same<T, T> = **true** ;

   It can be used like a variable:

   is_same<T, U>

Note that in C++14, template aliases like the following are incorporated:

```
1 template <class T, class U>
2     using is_same_t = typename is_same<T, U>::type;
```

0.15   auto variable template and generic lambda

** Question 15   auto variable template and generic lambda

Is this a valid code?

```
1 template<typename T>
2 auto f = [](auto a, T b){ /**/ };
3
4 int main()
5 {
6     f<int>(1, 2);
7 }
```

Solution of Question 15

Yes and it works as expected in C++14 and clang 3.5 trunk.

0.16 constexpr member functions and implicit const

*** Question 16 constexpr member functions and implicit const

Review the program :

```
1  #include <iostream>
2
3  struct A
4  {
5      constexpr A() : n(3) {}
6      constexpr int getN() const { return n; }
7
8      int n;
9  };
10
11
12 struct B
13 {
14     constexpr B() : a() {}
15     constexpr const A &getA() const
16     {
17         return a;
18     }
19     A &getA()
20     {
21         return a;
22     }
23
24     A a;
25 };
26
27
28 int main()
29 {
30
31     constexpr int n = B().getA().getN();
32 }
```

Solution of Question 16

Compiler error looks like:

```
constexpr_implicit_const.cpp: In function 'int main()':
constexpr_implicit_const.cpp:31:32:
error: call to non-constexpr function 'A& B::getA()'
    constexpr int n = B().getA().getN();
                        ^
```

B().getA() selects the non-constant overload version, leading to this error.
After rendering the code as :

```
1  #include <iostream>
2
3  struct A
4  {
5      constexpr A() : n(3) {}
6      constexpr int getN() const { return n; }
7
8      int n;
9  };
10
11
12 struct B
13 {
14     constexpr B() : a() {}
15     constexpr const A &getA() const
16     {
17         return a;
18     }
19     constexpr A &getA()
20     {
```

```
21          return a;
22      }
23
24      A a;
25 };
26
27
28 int main()
29 {
30
31      constexpr int n = B().getA().getN();
32 }
```

We get the following compiler error with C++11: clang++ -std=c++11

```
constexpr_implicit_const1.cpp:19:18:
warning: 'constexpr' non-static member
        function will not be implicitly 'const' in C++1y;
        add 'const' to avoid a
        change in behavior [-Wconstexpr-not-const]
     constexpr A &getA()
                  ^
                        const
constexpr_implicit_const1.cpp:19:18:
error: functions that differ only in their
        return type cannot be overloaded
constexpr_implicit_const1.cpp:15:24:
note: previous declaration is here
     constexpr const A &getA() const
                  ^
constexpr_implicit_const1.cpp:21:16:
error: binding of reference to type 'A' to
        a value of type 'const A' drops qualifiers
          return a;
                 ^

1 warning and 2 errors generated.
```

It points to a couple of issues including the restriction that *constexpr member functions are implicitly const in C++11* which creates problems for literal class types which desire to be usable both within constant expressions and outside them.

So in C++14, this rule is removed. So it works fine with C++14 compliant compiler like clang 3.5 trunk.

0.17 constexpr constructor and initialization

** Question 17   constexpr constructor and initialization

Review the program :

```
1 int x;
2
3 struct A
4 {
5      constexpr A(bool b) : m(b?42:x) { }
6      int m;
7 };
8
9 constexpr int v = A(true).m;
10
11 constexpr int w = A(false).m;
```

Solution of Question 17

Compiler error with gcc 4.9 trunk is:

```
constexpr_constructor.cpp:11:28:
in constexpr expansion of 'A(0)'
```

```
constexpr_constructor.cpp:11:28:
error: the value of 'x' is not usable in a constant expression
 constexpr int w = A(false).m;
                   ^
constexpr_constructor.cpp:1:5: note: 'int x' is not const
 int x;
     ^
```

Compiler error with clang 3.5 trunk is:

```
constexpr_constructor.cpp:11:15:
error: constexpr variable 'w' must be
       initialized by a constant expression
constexpr int w = A(false).m;
              ^   ~~~~~~~~~~
constexpr_constructor.cpp:5:34:
note: read of non-const variable 'x' is not
      allowed in a constant expression
    constexpr A(bool b) : m(b?42:x) { }
                                 ^
constexpr_constructor.cpp:11:19: note: in call to 'A(false)'
constexpr int w = A(false).m;
                  ^
constexpr_constructor.cpp:1:5: note: declared here
int x;
    ^
1 error generated.
```

The first call to constructor is ok it initializes m with the value 42 whereas the second call is in error because initializer for m is x, which is non-constant.

0.18 constexpr and branching

** Question 18   constexpr and branching

Can we use if-then-else version of the following constexpr factorial program:

```
1 constexpr unsigned long long fact( unsigned long long x )
2 {
3     return x <= 1 ? 1ull : x * fact(x−1);
4 }
```

Solution of Question 18

C++14 allowed constexpr to include branching, so we can rewrite as follows:

```
1 constexpr auto fact( unsigned long long x )
2 {
3     if( x <= 1 )
4         return 1ull;
5     else
6         return x * fact(x−1);
7 }
```

0.19 constexpr and looping iteration

** Question 19   constexpr and looping iteration

Can we use if-then-else version of the following constexpr factorial program:

```
1 constexpr unsigned long long fact( unsigned long long x )
2 {
3     return x <= 1 ? 1ull : x * fact(x−1);
4 }
```

Solution of Question 19

C++14 allowed constexpr to support loop constructs, so we can rewrite the factorial program in its iterative version as follows:

```
1 constexpr auto fact( unsigned long long x )
2 {
3     auto product = x;
4
5     while( −−x )
6         product *= x;
7
8     return product;
9 }
```

C++11 requirement that constexprs be single return statements worked well enough, but simple functions that required more than one line could not be constexpr. It sometimes forced inefficient implementations in order to have at least some of its results generated at compile-time, but not always all. So this limitation was removed in C++14.

Note that this version may be more efficient, both at compile time and run time.

0.20   constexpr and mutation

** Question 20   constexpr and mutation

Review the program:

```
1 constexpr int f(int k)
2 {
3     constexpr int x = k;
4     return x;
5 }
```

Solution of Question 20

It results into compiler error like:

```
constexpr_init.cpp:3:19:
error: constexpr variable 'x' must be initialized by a
       constant expression
    constexpr int x = k;
                    ^   ~
constexpr_init.cpp:3:23:
note: read of non-const variable 'k' is not allowed in
      a constant expression
    constexpr int x = k;
                    ^
constexpr_init.cpp:1:21: note: declared here
constexpr int f(int k)
                  ^

1 error generated.
```

The reason is : x is not initialized by a constant expression because lifetime of k began outside the initializer of x.

So the line

```
constexpr int x = k;
```

should be replaced by:

```
int x = k;
```

To understand it better, let us review the following program:

```
1 constexpr int incr(int &n)
2 {
3     return ++n;
4 }
5
6 constexpr int g(int k)
7 {
8     constexpr int x = incr(k);
9     return x;
10 }
```

Here also, $incr(k)$ is not a core constant expression because lifetime of k began outside the expression $incr(k)$, so the culprit line responsible for compiler error is:

```
1 constexpr int x = incr(k);
```

Note that the following program is valid:

```
1 constexpr int h(int k)
2 {
3     int x = incr(k);
4     return x;
5 }
6 constexpr int y = h(1);
```

Because $h(1)$ is a core constant expression because the lifetime of k begins inside $h(1)$. It initializes y with the value 2.

To summarize, C++14 allows *mutation of objects whose lifetime began within the constant expression evaluation.*

0.21 constexpr vs static vs uninitialized

** Question 21   constexpr vs static vs uninitialized

Review the program:

```
1 constexpr int first(int n)
2 {
3     static int value = n;
4     return value;
5 }
6
7 constexpr int uninit()
8 {
9     int a;
10    return a;
11 }
```

Solution of Question 21

It does not compile. Typical error is, which is self-explanatory:

```
constexpr_static.cpp:3:16:
error: static variable not permitted in a constexpr
       function
    static int value = n;
                 ^
constexpr_static.cpp:9:9:
error: variables defined in a constexpr function must
       be initialized
    int a;
        ^

2 errors generated.
```

0.22   constexpr vs member function revisited

** Question 22   constexpr vs member function revisited

Is this code valid in C++14 ?

```
1 struct S
2 {
3      constexpr const int &f();
4      int &f();
5 };
```

Solution of Question 22

It was valid in C++11, but no more valid in C++14 because *constexpr* non-static member functions are not implicitly const member functions anymore.

Rationale behind this change was *to allow constexpr member functions to mutate the object.*
So the error is because it declares the same member function twice with different return types.
Typical error is, which is self-explanatory:

```
constexpr_memfn.cpp:4:10:
error: functions that differ only in their return type
      cannot be overloaded
    int &f();
        ^

constexpr_memfn.cpp:3:26: note: previous declaration is here
    constexpr const int &f();
                        ^

1 error generated.
```

0.23   deprecated attribute

** Question 23   deprecated attribute

Describe a mechanism to mark the usage of the class *A* and the function *func1* deprecated.

```
1 class A1 {};
2
3 void func1() {}
4
5 int main()
6 {
7      A1 a;
8      func1();
9 }
```

Solution of Question 23

C++14 introduced an attribute *[[deprecated]]* to do the needful. So we can rewrite the above code as:

```
1 class [[deprecated]] A1 {};
2
3 [[deprecated]]
4 void func1() {}
5
6 int main()
7 {
8      A1 a;
9      func1();
10 }
```

Compiler diagnostic messages with clang 3.5 trunk :

```
deprecated_attribute.cpp:8:5: warning: 'A1' is deprecated
      [-Wdeprecated-declarations]
    A1 a;
    ^
deprecated_attribute.cpp:1:22:
note: 'A1' has been explicitly marked deprecated
      here
class [[deprecated]] A1 {};
                     ^
deprecated_attribute.cpp:9:5: warning: 'func1' is deprecated
      [-Wdeprecated-declarations]
    func1();
    ^
deprecated_attribute.cpp:4:6:
note: 'func1' has been explicitly marked
      deprecated here
void func1() {}
     ^

2 warnings generated.
```

With gcc 4.9 trunk:

```
deprecated_attribute.cpp: In function 'int main()':
deprecated_attribute.cpp:8:8:
warning: 'A1' is deprecated
(declared at deprecated_attribute.cpp:1)
[-Wdeprecated-declarations]
      A1 a;
       ^
deprecated_attribute.cpp:9:5:
warning: 'void func1()' is deprecated
(declared at deprecated_attribute.cpp:4)
[-Wdeprecated-declarations]
      func1();
      ^
deprecated_attribute.cpp:9:11:
warning: 'void func1()' is deprecated
(declared at deprecated_attribute.cpp:4)
 [-Wdeprecated-declarations]
      func1();
           ^
```

The diagnostic message can be customized by passing a literal string as an argument to *[[deprecated]]* like:

```
1 class [[deprecated("Usage of class A is deprecated. Please class X instead.
      ")]] A1 {};
2
3 [[deprecated("Usage of func1 is deprecated. Please use func2 instead.")]]
4 void func1() {}
5
6 int main()
7 {
8     A1 a;
9     func1();
10 }
```

gcc 4.9 trunk yields now:

```
deprecated_attribute_msg.cpp: In function 'int main()':
deprecated_attribute_msg.cpp:8:8:
warning: 'A1' is deprecated
(declared at deprecated_attribute_msg.cpp:1):
Usage of class A is deprecated. Please class X instead.
[-Wdeprecated-declarations]
```

```
    A1 a;
    ^
```

```
deprecated_attribute_msg.cpp:9:5:
warning: 'void func1()' is deprecated
(declared at deprecated_attribute_msg.cpp:4):
Usage of func1 is deprecated. Please use func2 instead.
[-Wdeprecated-declarations]
     func1();
     ^
```

```
deprecated_attribute_msg.cpp:9:11:
warning: 'void func1()' is deprecated
(declared at deprecated_attribute_msg.cpp:4):
Usage of func1 is deprecated. Please use func2 instead.
[-Wdeprecated-declarations]
      func1();
           ^
```

The attribute-token *deprecated* can be used to mark names and entities whose use is still allowed, but is discouraged for some reason.

The attribute may be applied to the declaration of

- a class,
- a typedef-name,
- a variable,
- a non-static data member,
- a function,
- an enumeration, or
- a template specialization.

A name or entity declared without the *deprecated* attribute can later be redeclared with the attribute and vice-versa.

```
1 class A;
2 class [[deprecated]] A;
3
4 class A{};
5
6 int main()
7 {
8     A a;
9 }
```

Compiler issues proper diagnostic.

Thus, an entity initially declared without the attribute can be marked as deprecated by a subsequent redeclaration.

However, after an entity is marked as deprecated, later redeclarations do not un-deprecate the entity.

So for the code below, compiler still issues the relevant diagnostics:

```
1 class [[deprecated]] A;
2 class A;
3
4 class A{};
5
6 int main()
7 {
8     A a;
9 }
```

Redeclarations using different forms of the attribute, with or without the attribute-argument-clause or with different attribute-argument-clauses) are allowed.

```
1 class [[deprecated]] A;
2 class [[deprecated("Do not use A.")]] A;
3 class [[deprecated("A is dangerous.")]] A;
4
5 class A{};
6
```

```
7 int main()
8 {
9     A a;
10 }
```

Compiler issues diagnostic message for the last one :

```
deprecated_redeclare.cpp:9:5:
warning: 'A' is deprecated: A is dangerous.
      [-Wdeprecated-declarations]
    A a;
    ^
deprecated_redeclare.cpp:5:7:
note: 'A' has been explicitly marked deprecated
      here
class A{};
      ^

1 warning generated.
```

0.24   Member initializers and aggregate class

*** Question 24   Member initializers and aggregates

What is the output of the program ?

```
1 #include <iostream>
2
3 struct Univ
4 {
5     std::string name;
6     int rank;
7     int i;
8     std::string city = "unknown";
9     char c = city[rank];
10 };
11
12 int main()
13 {
14     Univ u = {"Columbia", 3};
15
16     std::cout << u.name << ' ' << u.rank
17               << ' ' << u.i << ' '
18               << u.city << ' ' << u.c << '\n';
19 }
```

Solution of Question 24

Kindly note that the class *Univ* is an *aggregate* because it satisfies all the criteria enlisted ahead, it has

- no user-provided constructors,
- no private or protected non-static data members,
- no base classes,
- and no virtual functions

If there are fewer initializer-clauses in the list than there are members in the aggregate, then each member not explicitly initialized will be initialized from

- its brace-or-equal-initializer or,
- an empty initializer list if there is no brace-or-equal-initializer.

Hence

- *u.name* is initialized with *Columbia*,
- *u.rank* with 3,
- *u.i* with the value of an expression of the form *int{}()*, that is, 0
- *u.city* with *unknown*

- *u.c* with the value of *u.city[c.rank]*, i.e., with the character at the 3rd index of the string *unknown*, i.e., with *n*.

  To summarize, it prints:

```
Columbia 3 0 unknown n
```

0.25 Member initializers and aggregate array

*** Question 25   Member initializers and aggregates

Does *a* have two elements or three? Is it actually possible to override the default value for *k* ? What are the values of *a*[0].*k* and *a*[1].*k* ?

```
struct X { int i, j, k = 42; };

X a[] = { 1, 2, 3, 4, 5, 6 };
```

Solution of Question 25

Please note that the array *a* is an aggregate.

```
1 #include <iostream>
2
3 struct X { int i, j, k = 42; };
4
5 X a[] = { 1, 2, 3, 4, 5, 6 };
6
7 int main()
8 {
9     size_t len = sizeof(a)/sizeof(a[0]);
10
11    std::cout << "size of a is : " << len << std::endl;
12
13    std::cout << "a[0].k : " << a[0].k << std::endl;
14    std::cout << "a[1].k : " << a[1].k << std::endl;
15 }
```

It simply prints:

```
size of a is : 2
a[0].k : 3
a[1].k : 6
```

So *a* is equivalent to *b* :

```
X b[2] = { { 1, 2, 3 }, { 4, 5, 6 } };
```

0.26 Data Member initializers

*** Question 26   Data Member initializers

In the program below, how should *a.x.b* be initialized here ?

```
1 #include <iostream>
2
3 struct A
4 {
5     struct X { int a, b; };
6
7     X x = { 1, 2 };
8
9     int n;
10 };
11
12 int main()
13 {
14     A a = {{10}, 5};
15     std::cout << a.x.b << std::endl;
16 }
```

Solution of Question 26

Kindly note that we can only use a non-static data member initializer if the member is not explicitly initialized.

In this case, $a.x$ does have an initializer $\{10\}$, so the non-static data member initializer is ignored, resulting in $a.x.b$ having the value 0.

0.27 time duration literals

** Question 27   time duration literals

How to express *hours, minutes, seconds, milliseconds, microseconds* and *nanoseconds* as a suffix to the intended entities to enforce expressiveness?

Solution of Question 27

C++14 introduced appropriate *chrono literals* to apply user-defined *integer literals* by overloading the *operator ""*:

```
constexpr chrono::hours operator"" h(unsigned long long hours);
constexpr chrono::minutes operator"" min(unsigned long long minutes);
constexpr chrono::seconds operator"" s(unsigned long long sec);
constexpr chrono::milliseconds operator"" ms(unsigned long long msec);
constexpr chrono::microseconds operator"" us(unsigned long long usec);
constexpr chrono::nanoseconds operator"" ns(unsigned long long nsec);
```

The suffixes *h,min,s,ms,us,ns* denote duration values of the corresponding types *hours, minutes, seconds, miliseconds, microseconds* and *nanoseconds* respectively if they are applied to integral literals.

Note that these time duration literals reside in inline namespace *std::literals::chrono_literals* which are made available in the namespace *std::chrono_literals* too.

```
1  #include <chrono>
2  #include <type_traits>
3
4  int main()
5  {
6      using namespace std::chrono_literals;
7
8      auto a = 10h;
9      auto b = 2min;
10     auto c = 20s;
11     auto d = 10ms;
12     auto e = 20us;
13     auto f = 5ns;
14
15     static_assert(std::is_same<decltype(a), std::chrono::hours>::value, "");
16     static_assert(std::is_same<decltype(b), std::chrono::minutes>::value, "");
17     static_assert(std::is_same<decltype(c), std::chrono::seconds>::value, "");
18     static_assert(std::is_same<decltype(d), std::chrono::milliseconds>::value, "");
19     static_assert(std::is_same<decltype(e), std::chrono::microseconds>::value, "");
20     static_assert(std::is_same<decltype(f), std::chrono::nanoseconds>::value, "");
21  }
```

```
1  #include <chrono>
2  #include <type_traits>
3  #include <cassert>
4
5  int main()
6  {
7      using namespace std::literals::chrono_literals;
8
```

```
 9 //     Make sure the types are right
10     static_assert ( std::is_same<decltype( 3h    ), std::chrono::hours>::
           value, "" );
11     static_assert ( std::is_same<decltype( 3min ), std::chrono::minutes>::
           value, "" );
12     static_assert ( std::is_same<decltype( 3s    ), std::chrono::seconds>::
           value, "" );
13     static_assert ( std::is_same<decltype( 3ms  ), std::chrono::
           milliseconds>::value, "" );
14     static_assert ( std::is_same<decltype( 3us  ), std::chrono::
           microseconds>::value, "" );
15     static_assert ( std::is_same<decltype( 3ns  ), std::chrono::nanoseconds
           >::value, "" );
16
17     std::chrono::hours h = 4h;
18     assert ( h == std::chrono::hours(4) );
19     auto h2 = 4.0h;
20     assert ( h == h2 );
21
22     std::chrono::minutes min = 36min;
23     assert ( min == std::chrono::minutes(36) );
24     auto min2 = 36.0min;
25     assert ( min == min2 );
26
27     std::chrono::seconds s = 24s;
28     assert ( s == std::chrono::seconds(24) );
29     auto s2 = 24.0s;
30     assert ( s == s2 );
31
32     std::chrono::milliseconds ms = 247ms;
33     assert ( ms == std::chrono::milliseconds(247) );
34     auto ms2 = 247.0ms;
35     assert ( ms == ms2 );
36
37     std::chrono::microseconds us = 867us;
38     assert ( us == std::chrono::microseconds(867) );
39     auto us2 = 867.0us;
40     assert ( us == us2 );
41
42     std::chrono::nanoseconds ns = 645ns;
43     assert ( ns == std::chrono::nanoseconds(645) );
44     auto ns2 = 645.ns;
45     assert ( ns == ns2 );
46 }
```

Similarly, C++14 introduced string literal s in *std::literals::string_literals* and complex literals *i, il, i_f* in inline namespace *std::literals::complex_ literals* by providing appropriate overloads for the *operator* "":

```
basic_string<char> operator "" s(const char *str, size_t len);
```

Enabling usage like:

```
auto str = ''testing''s;
```

0.28 Expressing π multiplication

** Question 28   user defined literals

Define a convenient suffix like $\_\pi$ for expressing values of π.

Solution of Question 28

We need to define a proper *literal operator* to handle this like:

```
1 #include <iostream>
2 #include <iomanip>
3
4 template<typename T>
5 constexpr T pi = T(3.1415926535897932385);
```

```
6
7
8 constexpr long double operator "" _pi(long double x)
9 {
10     return pi<long double> * x;
11 }
12
13 constexpr long double operator "" _pi(unsigned long long int x)
14 {
15     return pi<long double> * x;
16 }
17
18 int main()
19 {
20     std::cout << std::setprecision(10);
21
22     auto a = 2_pi;
23     auto b = -3.5_pi;
24
25     std::cout << a << std::endl;
26     std::cout << b << std::endl;
27 }
```

0.29   Compile Time _binary Literal Operator

**** Question 29   Compile Time _binary Literal Operator

Provide a compile time implementation of a user defined binary literal, which would allow writing programs like :

```
int main()
{
    const unsigned long long b = 110_binary;
    std::cout << "b : " << std::hex << b << std::endl;
}
```

which should simply print as expected:

```
b : 6
```

Solution of Question 29

sizeof... operator allows one to know the size of a parameter pack at compile time, so the code looks like:

```
1 #include <iostream>
2 #include <type_traits>
3 #include <limits>
4
5 template <char... Digits>
6 struct binary_lit_impl
7 {
8     static_assert(! sizeof...(Digits),
9         "binary literal digits must be 0 or 1");
10    static constexpr unsigned long long value=0;
11 };
12
13 // If the next digit is zero, then compute the rest
14 template <char... Digits>
15 struct binary_lit_impl<'0',Digits...>
16 {
17    static constexpr unsigned long long value=binary_lit_impl<Digits...>::
            value;
18 };
19
20 // If the next digit is one, then shift 1 and compute the rest
21 template <char... Digits>
22 struct binary_lit_impl<'1',Digits...>
23 {
```

```
24    static constexpr unsigned long long value=
25    binary_lit_impl<Digits... >::value|(1ULL<<sizeof...( Digits ));
26 };
27
28
29 template <char...  Digits>
30 constexpr unsigned long long operator "" _binary()
31 {
32    return binary_lit_impl<Digits... >::value;
33 }
34
35
36 int main()
37 {
38    const unsigned long long b = 110_binary;
39    std::cout << "b : " << std::hex << b << std::endl;
40 }
```

Alternatively:

```
1 #include <iostream>
2
3 template<typename T>
4 constexpr T binary_lit_impl()
5 {
6    return 0;
7 }
8
9 template<typename T, char C, char... Digits>
10 constexpr T binary_lit_impl()
11 {
12    static_assert(C == '0' || C == '1', "not a valid binary number");
13    return binary_lit_impl<T, Digits... >() + ((C=='1') ? 1 : 0) * (1ULL <<
          sizeof...( Digits ));
14 }
15
16
17 template<char...  Digits>
18 constexpr unsigned long long operator "" _binary()
19 {
20    return binary_lit_impl<unsigned long long, Digits... >();
21 }
22
23 int main()
24 {
25    signed short a = 110_binary;
26    std::cout << a << std::endl;
27
28    return 0;
29 }
```

More elaborated code may look like:

```
1 #include <iostream>
2 #include <type_traits>
3 #include <limits>
4
5 template <unsigned long long val, typename... Integers>
6 struct SelectIntType;
7
8 template <unsigned long long val, typename TypeInt, typename... Integers>
9 struct SelectIntType<val, TypeInt, Integers... >
10    :
11 std::integral_constant<
12    typename std::conditional<
                          (val <= static_cast<unsigned long long>
13
14                              (std::numeric_limits<TypeInt >::max()))
15                          ),
16                          TypeInt,
17                          typename SelectIntType<
18                                  val, Integers... >::value_type
19                          >::type,
20                          val>
21 {};
```

```
22
23 template <unsigned long long val>
24 struct SelectIntType<val>:std::integral_constant<unsigned long long,val>
25 {};
26
27 template <char... Digits>
28 struct bitsImpl
29 {
30     static_assert(! sizeof...(Digits),
31         "binary literal digits must be 0 or 1");
32     static constexpr unsigned long long value=0;
33 };
34
35 template <char... Digits>
36 struct bitsImpl<'0',Digits...>
37 {
38     static constexpr unsigned long long value=bitsImpl<Digits...>::value;
39 };
40
41 template <char... Digits>
42 struct bitsImpl<'1',Digits...>
43 {
44     static constexpr unsigned long long value=
45     bitsImpl<Digits...>::value|(1ULL<<sizeof...(Digits));
46 };
47
48
49 template <char... Digits>
50 constexpr typename SelectIntType<bitsImpl<Digits...>::value,
51         int, unsigned, long, unsigned long, long long>::value_type
52 operator "" _binary()
53 {
54     return SelectIntType<bitsImpl<Digits...>::value,
55         int, unsigned, long, unsigned long, long long>::value;
56 }
57
58
59 template <char... Digits>
60 constexpr typename SelectIntType<bitsImpl<Digits...>::value,
61         long, unsigned long, long long>::value_type
62 operator "" _binaryl()
63 {
64     return SelectIntType<bitsImpl<Digits...>::value,
65         long, unsigned long, long long>::value;
66 }
67
68
69 template <char... Digits>
70 constexpr auto operator "" _binaryL()
71     -> decltype(operator "" _binaryl<Digits...>())
72 {
73     return operator "" _binaryl<Digits...>();
74 }
75
76
77 template <char... Digits>
78 constexpr typename SelectIntType<bitsImpl<Digits...>::value,
79         long long>::value_type
80 operator "" _binaryll()
81 {
82     return SelectIntType<bitsImpl<Digits...>::value,
83                         long long>::value;
84 }
85
86
87 template <char... Digits>
88 constexpr auto operator "" _binaryLL()
89     -> decltype(operator "" _binaryll<Digits...>())
90 {
91     return operator "" _binaryll<Digits...>();
92 }
93
94
```

```
95
96 template <char... Digits>
97 constexpr typename SelectIntType<bitsImpl<Digits... >:: value,
98          unsigned, unsigned long >:: value_type
99 operator "" _binaryu ()
100 {
101     return SelectIntType<bitsImpl<Digits... >:: value,
102                          unsigned, unsigned long >:: value;
103 }
104
105
106
107 template <char... Digits>
108 constexpr auto operator "" _binaryU ()
109     -> decltype(operator "" _binaryu<Digits... >())
110 {
111     return operator "" _binaryu<Digits... >();
112
113 }
114
115
116
117 template <char... Digits>
118 constexpr typename SelectIntType<bitsImpl<Digits... >:: value,
119                          unsigned long >:: value_type
120 operator "" _binaryul ()
121 {
122     return SelectIntType<bitsImpl<Digits... >:: value,
123                          unsigned long >:: value;
124 }
125
126
127
128 template <char... Digits>
129 constexpr auto operator "" _binaryUL ()
130     -> decltype(operator "" _binaryul<Digits... >())
131 {
132     return operator "" _binaryul<Digits... >();
133 }
134
135
136
137 template <char... Digits>
138 constexpr auto operator "" _binaryuL ()
139     -> decltype(operator "" _binaryul<Digits... >())
140 {
141     return operator "" _binaryul<Digits... >();
142 }
143
144
145
146 template <char... Digits>
147 constexpr auto operator "" _binaryUl ()
148     -> decltype(operator "" _binaryul<Digits... >())
149 {
150     return operator "" _binaryul<Digits... >();
151 }
152
153
154
155 template <char... Digits>
156 constexpr unsigned long long operator "" _binaryull ()
157 {
158     return bitsImpl<Digits... >:: value;
159 }
160
161
162
163 template <char... Digits>
164 constexpr unsigned long long operator "" _binaryULL ()
165 {
166     return bitsImpl<Digits... >:: value;
167 }
168
169
170
```

```
171 template <char ... Digits>
172 constexpr unsigned long long operator "" _binaryuLL()
173 {
174     return bitsImpl<Digits ... >::value;
175 }
176
177
178
179 template <char ... Digits>
180 constexpr unsigned long long operator "" _binaryUll()
181 {
182     return bitsImpl<Digits ... >::value;
183 }
184
185
186
187
188 int main()
189 {
190     auto a1 = 110_binary;
191     auto a2 = 110_binaryl;
192     auto a3 = 110_binaryL;
193     auto a4 = 110_binaryll;
194     auto a5 = 110_binaryu;
195     auto a6 = 110_binaryul;
196     auto a7 = 110_binaryUL;
197     auto a8 = 110_binaryUl;
198     auto a9 = 110_binaryuL;
199     auto a10 = 110_binaryull;
200     auto a11 = 110_binaryULL;
201     auto a12 = 110_binaryuLL;
202     auto a13 = 110_binaryUll;
203 }
```

0.30 Square Literal Operator

** Question 30   Square Literal Operator

Implement a literal with suffix _square that computes the square of a given number, so that it can be used like:

```
const long double num = 25.5_square;
```

Solution of Question 30

```
1 constexpr long double operator "" _square(long double num)
2 {
3   return num*num;
4 }
```

0.31 Type Transformation Aliases

** Question 31   Type Transformation Aliases

Simplify the code below:

```
template< class T >
using reference_t
    = typename conditional<
            is_reference<T>::value,
            T,
            typename add_lvalue_reference<T>::type
        >::type;
```

Solution of Question 31

In a template context, C++ requires that each metacall to a metafunction bear syntactic overhead in the form of an introductory *typename* keyword, as well as the suffixed *::type* as could be seen in the code snippet.

Fortunately, C++14 removes this burden by providing a set of template aliases for the library's Transformation Traits, for example:

```
template <bool b, class T, class F>
using conditional_t
    = typename conditional<b,T,F>::type;

template <class T>
using add_lvalue_reference_t
    = typename add_lvalue_reference<T>::type;
```

So, the code provided can be simplified to look like:

```
template< class T >
using reference_t
    = conditional_t<
            is_reference<T>::value,
            T,
            add_lvalue_reference_t<T>
    >;
```

In this light, further additions are:

- const-volatile modifications:

```
template <class T>
using remove_const_t = typename remove_const<T>::type;

template <class T>
using remove_volatile_t = typename remove_volatile<T>::type;

template <class T>
using remove_cv_t = typename remove_cv<T>::type;

template <class T>
using add_const_t = typename add_const<T>::type;

template <class T>
using add_volatile_t = typename add_volatile<T>::type;

template <class T>
using add_cv_t = typename add_cv<T>::type;
```

- reference modifications:

```
template <class T>
using remove_reference_t
    = typename remove_reference<T>::type;

template <class T>
using add_lvalue_reference_t = typename add_lvalue_reference<T>::type;

template <class T>
using add_rvalue_reference_t = typename add_rvalue_reference<T>::type;
```

- sign modifications:

```
template <class T>
using make_signed_t
    = typename make_signed<T>::type;

template <class T>
using make_unsigned_t = typename make_unsigned<T>::type;
```

- array modifications:

```
template <class T>
using remove_extent_t
    = typename remove_extent<T>::type;

template <class T>
using remove_all_extents_t = typename remove_all_extents<T>::type;
```

- pointer modifications:

  ```
  template <class T>
  using remove_pointer_t = typename remove_pointer<T>::type;
  ```

  ```
  template <class T>
  using add_pointer_t
  = typename add_pointer<T>::type;
  ```

- other transformations:

  ```
  template <size_t Len, std::size_t Align>
  using aligned_storage_t = typename aligned_storage<Len,Align>::type;
  ```

  ```
  template <std::size_t Len, class... Types>
  using aligned_union_t = typename aligned_union<Len,Types...>::type;
  ```

  ```
  template <class T>
  using decay_t = typename decay<T>::type;
  ```

  ```
  template <bool b, class T=void>
  using enable_if_t = typename enable_if<b,T>::type;
  ```

  ```
  template <bool b, class T, class F>
  using conditional_t = typename conditional<b,T,F>::type;
  ```

  ```
  template <class... T>
  using common_type_t = typename common_type<T...>::type;
  ```

  ```
  template <class T>
  using underlying_type_t = typename underlying_type<T>::type;
  ```

  ```
  template <class T>
  using result_of_t = typename result_of<T>::type;
  ```

0.32   unique_ptr vs make_unique as function argument

*** Question 32   unique_ptr vs make_unique as function argument

Review the code below :

```
1 #include <iostream>
2
3 template<typename T1, typename T2>
4 void f(T1 * a, T2 * b)
5 {}
6
7 struct A
8 {
9     A() { std::cout << "A()" << std::endl; }
10    ~A() { std::cout << "~A()" << std::endl; }
11 };
12
13 struct B
14 {
15    B() { std::cout << "B()" << std::endl; }
16    ~B() { std::cout << "~B()" << std::endl; }
17 };
18
19 int main()
20 {
21    f(new A, new B);
22 }
```

Solution of Question 32

Suppose there is no exception raised, then the memories allocate by the calls *new A* and *new B* are leaked as can seen in the output of the program :

```
A()
B()
```

The destructors are not called. Classic memory leak. Moreover it suffers from problems associated with unspecified order of evaluation of the parameters to the function as depicted ahead.

Immediate Remedy: As a quick fix, suppose the code is modified to use *std::unique_ptr* instead of raw pointers:

```cpp
1  #include <iostream>
2  #include <memory>
3
4  template<typename T1, typename T2>
5  void f(std::unique_ptr<T1> a, std::unique_ptr<T2> b)
6  {}
7
8  struct A
9  {
10     A() { std::cout << "A()" << std::endl; }
11     ~A() { std::cout << "~A()" << std::endl; }
12 };
13
14 struct B
15 {
16     B() { std::cout << "B()" << std::endl; }
17     ~B() { std::cout << "~B()" << std::endl; }
18 };
19
20 int main()
21 {
22     f(std::unique_ptr<A>(new A), std::unique_ptr<B>(new B));
23 }
```

It prints now:

```
A()
B()
~B()
~A()
```

So no leak this time ! Is it ?

The order of evaluation of the parameters being passed to the function is unspecified. And we know that the call to *new A* invokes at least 2 different calls : *operator new* to allocate the memory followed by the call to A's constructor. Same is for *B*.

Let us assume that the evaluation of unique_ptr's construction occur last.

Suppose, *new A* succeeds and while evaluating *new B*, either the operator new of the call to B's constructor raises some exception, then A's memory will be leaked. Same is for *B*.

Suppose, the evaluation is like this : operator new gets called for A followed by B, the A's constructor gets called followed by B. If either A's or B's constructor fails then B's or A's memory is leaked respectively.

Hence in case of any exception during the evaluation of the parameters, there are possibilities of memory leak due to unspecified evaluation order of the expressions used as parameters.

So all we want is to provide a function template with perfect forwarding (because the user will be passing new from outside this function template) that does the work of allocation and construction of the object and construction of the unique_ptr.

Luckily, C++14 provides a perfectly forwarding variadic function template *std::make_unique*. Hence, the final code looks like :

```cpp
1  #include <iostream>
2  #include <memory>
3
4  template<typename T1, typename T2>
5  void f(std::unique_ptr<T1> a, std::unique_ptr<T2> b)
6  {}
7
8  struct A
9  {
10     A() { std::cout << "A()" << std::endl; }
11     ~A() { std::cout << "~A()" << std::endl; }
12 };
13
14 struct B
15 {
```

```cpp
16      B() { std::cout << "B()" << std::endl; }
17      ~B() { std::cout << "~B()" << std::endl; }
18 };
19
20 int main()
21 {
22      f(std::make_unique<A>(), std::make_unique<B>());
23 }
```

make_unique prevents the unspecified evaluation order leak triggered by the expression

```cpp
f(std::unique_ptr<A>(new A), std::unique_ptr<B>(new B));
```

Because, now the parameters are 2 functions, which will be executed irrespective of the order of evaluation.

Suppose the first call succeeds and the second call fails(i.e. throws) then the temporary object created by the first call is guaranteed to clean up because *temporary objects are destroyed as the last step in evaluating the full-expression that (lexically) contains the point where they were created. This is true even if that evaluation ends in throwing an exception.*

If the first call throws, then there are no leaks because *std::make_unique* is itself strongly exception-safe.

0.33   make_unique as perfect forwarding guy

** Question 33   make_unique as perfect forwarding guy

In the code below, we end up typing the name of the type *UserDefinedLongTypeName* twice:

```cpp
std::unique_ptr<UserDefinedLongTypeName> up(new UserDefinedLongTypeName());
```

How to resolve this ? Briefly describe the mechanism.

Solution of Question 33

As already mentioned before, the code can be rewritten as:

```cpp
auto up = std::make_unique<UserDefinedLongTypeName>();
```

So it helps us get rid of explicit call to *new* as well.

Mechanism : *make_unique< T >(args...)* invokes *new T(std::forward< Args >(args)...)*

And please note that this meant *T(params)* with parentheses rather than *T{params}*. If *T{params}* was adopted then the output of the following program will be 2 instead of 2014:

```cpp
auto up_vec1 = std::make_unique<std::vector<int>>(2014, 2017);
```

```cpp
std::cout << "size of the first vector is : " << up_vec1->size() << std::endl;
```

0.34   make_unique and new

*** Question 34   make_unique and new

Does *make_unique* calls plain *new* or global *new* ?

Solution of Question 34

As we know that the class template *default_delete* serves as the default deleter (destruction policy) for the class template *unique_ptr*.

default_delete provides the function call operator as follows :

```cpp
void operator()(T* ptr) const;
```

Effect of which is to calls plain delete on *ptr*. That's why *make_unique* also makes call to plain new, the matching guy, instead of the global one.

Please note that *make_shared< T >()* makes call to the global *new* as *::new (ptr)*. The reason is simple : it must invoke *true placement new*, which can't be replaced, instead of the following which is allowed to exist as well:

`T::operator new(size_t, void *)`

Similar behavior can be observed in this program:

```
1 #include <iostream>
2 #include <memory>
3 #include <cstdlib>
4
5 void* operator new(std::size_t s)
6 {
7     std::cout << "global operator new called" << std::endl;
8     return std::malloc(s);
9 }
10
11 void operator delete(void* ptr) noexcept
12 {
13     std::cout << "global operator delete called" << std::endl;
14     std::free(ptr);
15 }
16
17 struct A
18 {
19     A() { std::cout << "A's constructor called" << std::endl; }
20     ~A() { std::cout << "A's destructor called" << std::endl; }
21
22     static void* operator new(std::size_t s)
23     {
24         std::cout << "custom operator new called" << '\n';
25         return ::operator new(s);
26     }
27
28     static void operator delete(void * ptr)
29     {
30         std::cout << "custom operator delete called" << '\n';
31         ::operator delete(ptr);
32     }
33
34 };
35
36 int main()
37 {
38     std::cout << "Unique Pointer Start" << std::endl;
39     std::make_unique<A>();
40     std::cout << "Unique Pointer End" << '\n' << '\n';
41
42     std::cout << "Shared Pointer Start" << std::endl;
43     std::make_shared<A>();
44     std::cout << "Shared Pointer End" << std::endl;
45 }
```

As expected, it prints:

```
Unique Pointer Start
custom operator new called
global operator new called
A's constructor called
A's destructor called
custom operator delete called
global operator delete called
Unique Pointer End

Shared Pointer Start
global operator new called
A's constructor called
A's destructor called
global operator delete called
Shared Pointer End
```

0.35   make_unique and value initialization

*** Question 35   make_unique and value initialization

Given zero arguments, does *make_unique* make call to *new T()* for *value-initialization* or to *new T* for *default-initialization* ?

Solution of Question 35

It makes call to *new T()* for *value-initialization* because of the following reasons:
- symmetry with make_shared< *T* > (),
- consistency with the empty parentheses in the function call make_unique< *T* > (),
- predictability because this is the expected result of a variadic implementation, and
- safety because it is safe to get zero instead of garbage. *"zero is a strict subset of garbage"*.

Occasionally, the use may be interested in default-initialization due to performance. We already know that make_unique< *T* > () is faster than make_shared< *T* > (), but quite often the cost of a dynamic memory allocation plus the corresponding deallocation is much higher than the cost of value-initializing a single object.

0.36   make_unique and single object

*** Question 36   make_unique and single object

Illustrate the mechanism to manage single object's dynamic memory with *make_unique*.

Solution of Question 36

Let us take a simple example:

```cpp
#include <memory>
#include <cassert>

struct A
{
    A() : b(false) { }
    A(int, double&, char&&, void*) : b(true) { }
    bool b;
};

int main()
{
    int i = 0;
    double d = 0.0;
    char c = 0;

    std::unique_ptr<A> a = std::make_unique<A>(i, d, std::move(c), nullptr);

    assert( a != nullptr );
    assert( a->b );

    a = std::make_unique<A>();
    assert( a != nullptr );
    assert( !a->b );
}
```

It works as expected, all asserts are true.
    Same is the case for the following example:

```cpp
#include <memory>
#include <string>
#include <cassert>

int main()
{
    std::unique_ptr<int> p1 = std::make_unique<int>(100);
    assert ( *p1 == 100 );
```

```
10      p1 = std :: make_unique<int> ();
11      assert ( *p1 == 0 );
12
13
14      std :: unique_ptr<std :: string> p2 = std :: make_unique<std :: string> ( "
           Chandra" );
15      assert ( *p2 == "Chandra" );
16
17      p2 = std :: make_unique<std :: string> ();
18      assert ( *p2 == "" );
19
20      p2 = std :: make_unique<std :: string> ( 10, 'c' );
21      assert ( *p2 == "cccccccccc" );
22 }
```

To understand the mechanism better, let us go through the implementation details of *make_unique* as far as managing single object's memory is concerned.

Let us recall the interface :

template<**class** T, **class** ... Args> unique_ptr<T> make_unique(Args&&... args);

And the implementation looks like:

```
1 template<typename T, typename ... Args>
2 inline  unique_ptr<T> make_unique(Args&&... args)
3 {
4      return unique_ptr<T>(new T(std :: forward<Args>(args) ...));
5 }
```

0.37   make_unique and default initialization

** Question 37   make_unique and default initialization

Write a function which would do the default initialization with *make_unique* as far as managing single object's memory is concerned.

Solution of Question 37

```
1 template<class T>
2 inline  unique_ptr<T> make_unique_default_init ()
3 {
4      return unique_ptr<T>(new T) ;
5 }
```

To understand it better, let us recall certain concepts like default initialization, value initialization and zero initialization.

- *zero initialization* :
  - if T is a scalar type, the object is initialized to the value obtained by converting the integer literal 0 (zero) to T.
  - if T is a (possibly cv-qualified) non-union class type, each non-static data member and each base-class subobject is zero-initialized and padding is initialized to zero bits.
  - if T is a (possibly cv-qualified) union type, the object's first non-static named data member is zero-initialized and padding is initialized to zero bits.
  - if T is an array type, each element is zero-initialized.
  - if T is a reference type, no initialization is performed.

- *default initialization* :
  - if T is a (possibly cv-qualified) class type, the default constructor for T is called and the initialization is ill-formed if T has no default constructor or overload resolution results in an ambiguity or in a function that is deleted or inaccessible from the context of the initialization.
  - if T is an array type, each element is default-initialized.
  - otherwise, no initialization is performed.

If a program calls for the default initialization of an object of a const-qualified type T, T shall be a class type with a user-provided default constructor.

- *value initialization* :

  − if T is a (possibly cv-qualified) class type with either no default constructor or a default constructor that is user-provided or deleted, then the object is default-initialized.

  − if T is a (possibly cv-qualified) class type without a user-provided or deleted default constructor, then the object is zero-initialized and the semantic constraints for default-initialization are checked, and if T has a non-trivial default constructor, the object is default-initialized.

  − if T is an array type, then each element is value-initialized.

  − otherwise, the object is zero-initialized.

  An object that is value-initialized is deemed to be constructed and thus labeled as *constructed* objects, objects for which the constructor has completed, etc., even if no constructor is invoked for the object's initialization.

A program that calls for default-initialization or value-initialization of an entity of reference type is ill-formed. Every object of static storage duration is zero-initialized at program startup before any other initialization takes place.

An object whose initializer is an empty set of parentheses, i.e., (), shall be value-initialized. Since () is not permitted by the syntax for initializer, the following is not the declaration of an object of class X, but the declaration of a function taking no argument and returning an X:

X a ( ) ;

If no initializer is specified for an object, the object is default-initialized. If no initialization is performed, an object with automatic or dynamic storage duration has indeterminate value. Objects with static or thread storage duration are zero-initialized.

If the initializer is (), the object is value-initialized.

0.38   make_unique and array T[n]

*** Question 38   make_unique and array T[n]

What is the output of the program ?

```cpp
#include <memory>
#include <iostream>

int main ()
{
    auto up = std :: make_unique<int [5] >() ;

    for (int  i = 0;  i < 5;  ++i )
    {
        std :: cout << up[ i ] << " ";
    }
    std :: cout << std :: endl;
}
```

Solution of Question 38

It does not get compiled. Error with gcc 4.9 looks like:

```
make_unique_array1.cpp:6:40:
error: use of deleted function
'typename std::_MakeUniq<_Tp>::__invalid_type
std::make_unique(_Args&& ...)
[with _Tp = int [5]; _Args = {};
typename std::_MakeUniq<_Tp>::__invalid_type
= std::_MakeUniq<int [5]>::__invalid_type]'
     auto up = std::make_unique<int[5]>();
                                        ^
In file included from
```

```
/usr/local/include/c++/4.9.0/memory:81:0,
              from make_unique_array1.cpp:1:
/usr/local/include/c++/4.9.0/bits/unique_ptr.h:773:5:
note: declared here
     make_unique(_Args&&...) = delete;
     ^
```

This error brings forth the point that *std::make_unique* is disabled for arrays of known bound, $T == U[N]$:

template <**class** T, **class**... Args> unspecified make_unique(Args&&...) = **delete**;

To understand the return type *unspecified* better, let us dive a bit into the implementation details :

```
 1 template<class T>
 2 struct unique_type
 3 {
 4     typedef unique_ptr<T> single_object;
 5 };
 6
 7 template<class T, size_t N>
 8 struct unique_type<T[N]>
 9 {
10     typedef void array_known_bound;
11 };
12
13 template<class T, class... Args>
14 typename unique_type<T>::array_known_bound
15     make_unique(Args&&...) = delete;
```

Alternatively, we can define *array_known_bound* to be an empty struct instead of typedef to *void*.

Rationale for disabling T[n]

As of now, *unique_ptr* doesn't provide a partial specialization for $T[n]$.

However, users will be strongly tempted to write *make_unique< $T[n]$ > ()*.

- Returning *unique_ptr< $T[N]$ >* would select the primary template for single objects, which is bizarre.
- Returning *unique_ptr< $T[]$ >* would be an exception to the otherwise ironclad rule that *make_unique< something > ()* returns *unique_ptr< something >*.

Therefore, $T[N]$ is disabled.

Alternatively, $T[N]$ can be made ill-formed as well:

```
 1 template<class T> struct Never_True : std::false_type { };
 2
 3 template<class T>
 4 struct unique_type
 5 {
 6     typedef unique_ptr<T> single_object;
 7 };
 8
 9 template<class T, size_t N> struct unique_type<T[N]>
10 {
11         static_assert(Never_True<T>::value, "make_unique forbids T[N].
              Please use T[].");
12 };
```

0.39   make_unique and array T[]

*** Question 39   make_unique and array T[]

Rewrite the previous program. Describe how *make_unique* works with arrays of runtime length.

Solution of Question 39

```cpp
#include <memory>
#include <iostream>

int main()
{
    auto up = std::make_unique<int[]>(5);

    for(int i = 0; i < 5; ++i)
    {
        std::cout << up[i] << " ";
    }
    std::cout << std::endl;
}
```

It prints:

0 0 0 0 0

Implementation may look like :

```cpp
template<class T>
struct unique_type
{
    typedef unique_ptr<T> single_object;
};

template<class T>
struct unique_type<T[]>
{
    typedef unique_ptr<T[]> array_unknown_bound;
};

template<class T>
typename unique_type<T>::array_unknown_bound
make_unique(size_t n)
{
    typedef typename std::remove_extent<T>::type Up;

    return unique_ptr<T>(new Up[n]());
}
```

We could drop the typedef and just get one-liner for the function body :

```cpp
template<class T>
typename unique_type<T>::array_unknown_bound
make_unique(size_t n)
{
    return unique_ptr<T>(new typename std::remove_extent<T>::type[n]());
}
```

Let us put forth another example to illustrate its usage(it runs fine):

```cpp
#include <memory>
#include <cassert>

struct A
{
    A() : b(true) { }
    A(int) : b(false) { }
    bool b;
};


int main()
{
    std::unique_ptr<A[]> a = std::make_unique<A[]>(3);
    assert( a != nullptr );
    assert( a[0].b && a[1].b && a[2].b );
}
```

Similarly, the following calls are invalid ones leading to compiler errors:

```
1 struct A { };
2
3 // no matching function
4 auto p1 = std::make_unique<A[]>();
5
6 // no matching function
7 auto p2 = std::make_unique<A[]>(1, 2);
8
9
10 // deleted
11 auto p3 = std::make_unique<A[1]>();
12 auto p4 = std::make_unique<A[1]>(1);
13 auto p4 = std::make_unique<A[1]>(1, 2);
```

To summarize, *make_unique< T[]>(n)* invokes *new T[n]()*, requesting value-initialization.

0.40   make_unique and default initialization with T[]

** Question 40   make_unique and default initialization with T[]

How would you support default initialization with T[] when called with *make_unique*?

Solution of Question 40

It is very simple. We just need to replace the call to *new T[n]()* with *new T[n]*.
To elaborate, the code with value initialization is:

```
1 template<class T>
2 typename unique_type<T>::array_unknown_bound
3 make_unique(size_t n)
4 {
5     return unique_ptr<T>(new typename std::remove_extent<T>::type[n]());
6 }
```

With this, the code below will value initialize the array, i.e., all the five elements of the array will be having values as zero:

```
make_unique<int[]>(5);
```

And, the code with default initialization will be:

```
1 template<class T>
2 typename unique_type<T>::array_unknown_bound
3 make_unique(size_t n)
4 {
5     return unique_ptr<T>(new typename std::remove_extent<T>::type[n]);
6 }
```

With this, the code below will default initialize the array, i.e., all the five elements of the array will be carrying some garbage values:

```
make_unique<int[]>(5);
```

With this change, the following code will also default initialize the integer with some garbage value:

```
make_unique<int>();
```

0.41   Extend make_unique : Support list initialization T[]

*** Question 41   Extend make_unique : Support list initialization T[]

As of now, *make_unique* does not list initialization, so the following is not possible:

```
1 make_unique_auto_size<int[]>(1, 2, 3, 4, 5);
```

which value initializes the integer array with list of values supplied.

Develop an utility to achieve this.

Solution of Question 41

Based on our experience of *make_unique* so far, it was not difficult to take a byte of this extension.

```cpp
#include <memory>
#include <type_traits>
#include <iostream>

template<class T, class... Args>
typename std::unique_ptr<T[]>
make_unique_deduce_length(Args&&... args)
{
        return std::unique_ptr<T>(new typename std::remove_extent<T>::type[
                sizeof...(Args)]{ std::forward<Args>(args)... });
}


int main()
{
    auto up = make_unique_deduce_length<int[]>(1, 2, 3, 4, 5);

    for (int i = 0; i < 5; ++i)
    {
        std::cout << up[i] << " ";
    }
    std::cout << std::endl;
}
```

Alas, this didn't compile. Compiler error is:

```
make_unique_utils.cpp:15:15:
 error: no matching function for call to
     'make_unique_deduce_length'
   auto up = make_unique_deduce_length<int[]>(1, 2, 3, 4, 5);
             ^~~~~~~~~~~~~~~~~~~~~~~~~~~~
make_unique_utils.cpp:7:1:
note: candidate template ignored:
substitution failure [with T = int []]:
array has incomplete element type 'int []'
make_unique_deduce_length(Args&&... args)
^

1 error generated.
```

Because *int []* is an incomplete type, hence *sizeof* cannot be applied to it. So we need to find a way to circumvent this:

```cpp
#include <memory>
#include <type_traits>
#include <iostream>

template<class T>
struct unique_type
{
    typedef std::unique_ptr<T> single_object;
};

template<class T>
struct unique_type<T[]>
{
    typedef std::unique_ptr<T[]> array_unknown_bound;
};

template<class T, class... Args>
typename unique_type<T>::array_unknown_bound
make_unique_deduce_length(Args&&... args)
{
        return std::unique_ptr<T>(new typename std::remove_extent<T>::type[
                sizeof...(Args)]{ std::forward<Args>(args)... });
```

```
22 }
23
24
25 int main ()
26 {
27     auto up = make_unique_deduce_length<int []>(1, 2, 3, 4, 5);
28
29     for (int i = 0; i < 5; ++i)
30     {
31         std::cout << up[i] << " ";
32     }
33     std::cout << std::endl;
34 }
```

which prints:

1 2 3 4 5

0.42   Extend make_unique : Value Initialize T[]

*** Question 42   Extend make_unique : Value Initialize T[]

Develop an utility *make_unique_value_init< T[]>(n, args...)*, which will do value-initialization for extra elements at the end, so writing code like this is possible:

make_unique_value_init<int []>(5, 100, 200, 300);

which will create an integer array of length five and first three elements initialized to 100, 200, 300 respectively. Last two elements are value initialized to T(), i.e., int(), i.e., to zero.

Solution of Question 42

```
1 #include <memory>
2 #include <type_traits>
3 #include <iostream>
4
5 template<class T>
6 struct unique_type
7 {
8     typedef std::unique_ptr<T> single_object;
9 };
10
11 template<class T>
12 struct unique_type<T[]>
13 {
14     typedef std::unique_ptr<T[]> array_unknown_bound;
15 };
16
17 template<class T, class... Args>
18 typename unique_type<T>::array_unknown_bound
19 make_unique_value_init(size_t n, Args&&... args)
20 {
21         return std::unique_ptr<T>(new typename std::remove_extent<T>::type[
                n]{std::forward<Args>(args)... });
22 }
23
24
25 int main ()
26 {
27     auto up = make_unique_value_init<int []>(5, 100, 200, 300);
28
29     for (int i = 0; i < 5; ++i)
30     {
31         std::cout << up[i] << " ";
32     }
33     std::cout << std::endl;
34 }
```

which prints:

```
100 200 300 0 0
```

Note that providing zero elements makes this equivalent to the existing *make_unique*, i.e., the following two lines are doing equivalent jobs:

```
make_unique_value_init<int[]>(5);
std::make_unique<int[]>(5);
```

0.43   Extend make_unique : T[N]

*** Question 43   Extend make_unique : T[N]

Develop an utility which will allow *unique_ptr* to work with arrays of a given extent N, T[N].

Solution of Question 43

```
1 #include <memory>
2 #include <type_traits>
3 #include <iostream>
4
5 template<class T>
6 struct unique_type
7 {
8       typedef std::unique_ptr<T> single_object;
9 };
10
11 template<class T, std::size_t N>
12 struct unique_type<T[N]>
13 {
14       typedef std::unique_ptr<T[]> fixed_array;
15
16       template <typename... Args>
17       static inline fixed_array make(Args&&... args)
18       {
19            static_assert(N >= sizeof...(Args),
20            "make_unique<T[N]> : no of arguments can't be more than N");
21            return fixed_array(new T[N]{std::forward<Args>(args)...});
22       }
23 };
24
25 template<typename T, class... Args>
26 typename unique_type<T>::fixed_array
27 make_unique_fixed_array(Args&&... args)
28 {
29       return unique_type<T>::make(std::forward<Args>(args)...);
30 }
31
32
33 int main()
34 {
35       auto up = make_unique_fixed_array<int[5]>();
36
37       for (int i = 0; i < 5; ++i)
38       {
39            std::cout << up[i] << " ";
40       }
41       std::cout << std::endl;
42
43       auto up1 = make_unique_fixed_array<int[5]>(1, 2);
44
45       for (int i = 0; i < 5; ++i)
46       {
47            std::cout << up1[i] << " ";
48       }
49       std::cout << std::endl;
50
51       auto up2 = make_unique_fixed_array<int[5]>(1, 2, 3, 4, 5);
52
53       for (int i = 0; i < 5; ++i)
```

```
54    {
55        std::cout << up2[i] << " ";
56    }
57    std::cout << std::endl;
58 }
```

which prints:

```
0 0 0 0 0
1 2 0 0 0
1 2 3 4 5
```

Whereas the call below will result into compiler error as expected by static_assert message:

```
auto up = make_unique_fixed_array<int[5]>(1, 2, 3, 4, 5, 6);
```

Error may look like:

```
make_unique_utils4.cpp:19:9:
error: static_assert failed "make_unique<T[N]> : no
    of arguments can't be more than N"
      static_assert(N >= sizeof...(Args),
      ^             ~~~~~~~~~~~~~~~~~~~~~
make_unique_utils4.cpp:29:28:
note: in instantiation of function template
    specialization 'unique_type<int [5]>::
    make<int, int, int, int, int, int>'
    requested here
  return unique_type<T>::make(std::forward<Args>(args)...);
                       ^
make_unique_utils4.cpp:35:15:
note: in instantiation of function template
    specialization 'make_unique_fixed_array<
    int [5], int, int, int, int, int, int>' requested here
  auto up = make_unique_fixed_array<int[5]>(1, 2, 3, 4, 5, 6);
            ^
1 error generated.
```

0.44 allocate_unique

**** Question 44   allocate_unique

std::shared_ptr provides *std::allocate_shared*, but *std::unique_ptr* does not provide *std::allocate_unique* as of this writing. But some users may like to use their own custom allocator to make *unique_ptr*. Provide a suitable implementation for generic *allocate_unique* without modifying the implementation of *unique_ptr*.

Solution of Question 44

It is understood that the case of *allocate_unique* is entirely different from *std::allocate_shared*. Rather than going into much details, we would like to highlight key points:

- *make_shared* and *allocate_shared* incorporate optimization tricks under the hood to do things which is not easy for the user to do it herself.
- *shared_ptr* uses *allocate_shared* to help it allocate the reference counter, deleter and the shared object whereas *unique_ptr* manages just the object.
- The case of *allocate_unique* is unlike *allocate_shared*, because *shared_ptr* is powered by type erasure. So it has to be carefully designed as far as return type of *allocate_unique* is concerned.
- We cannot use default deleter, so design of an appropriate deleter is required.
- *shared_ptr* doesn't deal with arrays whereas *unique_ptr* deals with arrays. *allocate_unique* has to keep this into account, similar in line of *make_unique*.
- Writing a perfectly forwarding variadic templates could be tedious.

Keeping these points in mind, following are two implementation of *allocate_unique*:

First Implementation

```cpp
#include <memory>
#include <iostream>

template<typename Allocator>
struct alloc_deleter
{
  alloc_deleter(const Allocator& a) : a(a) { }

  typedef typename std::allocator_traits<Allocator>::pointer pointer;

  void operator()(pointer p) const
  {
    Allocator aa(a);
    std::allocator_traits<Allocator>::destroy(aa, std::addressof(*p));
    std::allocator_traits<Allocator>::deallocate(aa, p, 1);
  }

private:
  Allocator a;
};

template<typename T, typename Allocator, typename... Args>
auto
allocate_unique(const Allocator& alloc, Args&&... args)
{
  using AT = std::allocator_traits<Allocator>;
  static_assert(std::is_same<typename AT::value_type, std::remove_cv_t<T
      >>{}(),
                "Allocatorator has incorrect value_type");

  Allocator a(alloc);
  auto p = AT::allocate(a, 1);
  try {
    AT::construct(a, std::addressof(*p), std::forward<Args>(args)...);
    using D = alloc_deleter<Allocator>;
    return std::unique_ptr<T, D>(p, D(a));
  }
  catch (...)
  {
    AT::deallocate(a, p, 1);
    throw;
  }
}


struct A
{
  A() {std::cout << "A() called\n";}
  ~A() {std::cout << "~A() called\n";}

  void f() {std::cout << "A::f() called\n";}
};


int main()
{
  auto up = allocate_unique<A>(std::allocator<A>());
  up->f();

  std::allocator<int> a;
  auto p = allocate_unique<int>(a, 0);
  return *p;
}
```

It prints :
```
A() called
A::f() called
~A() called
```

Second Implementation

```
1  #include <type_traits>
2  #include <utility>
3  #include <memory>
4  #include <iostream>
5
6
7  template <class T>
8  inline T* to_raw_pointer(T* p) noexcept
9  {
10     return p;
11 }
12
13
14 template <class Pointer>
15 inline typename std::pointer_traits<Pointer>::element_type*
16 to_raw_pointer(Pointer p) noexcept
17 {
18     return to_raw_pointer(p.operator->());
19 }
20
21
22 template <class Allocator>
23 struct alloc_deleter : Allocator
24 {
25 public:
26     typedef Allocator allocator_type;
27     typedef std::allocator_traits<allocator_type> traits;
28     typedef typename traits::pointer pointer;
29
30     explicit alloc_deleter(const allocator_type& a)
31         : allocator_type(a) {}
32
33     void operator()(pointer p)
34     {
35         traits::destroy(*this, to_raw_pointer(p));
36         traits::deallocate(*this, p, 1);
37     }
38 };
39
40
41 template <class T, class Allocator, class ...Args>
42 std::unique_ptr<T, alloc_deleter<Allocator>>
43 allocate_unique(const Allocator& a, Args&& ...args)
44 {
45     typedef alloc_deleter<Allocator> A;
46     static_assert(sizeof(T) == sizeof(typename A::value_type),
47                   "Allocatorator has incorrect value_type");
48     A alloc(a);
49     auto p = std::allocator_traits<A>::allocate(alloc, 1);
50     try
51     {
52         std::allocator_traits<A>::construct(
53             alloc, to_raw_pointer(p), std::forward<Args>(args)...
54                                         );
55     }
56     catch (...)
57     {
58         std::allocator_traits<A>::deallocate(alloc, p, 1);
59         throw;
60     }
61     return std::unique_ptr<T, A>(p, alloc);
62 }
63
64
65 struct A
66 {
67     A() {std::cout << "A() called \n";}
68     ~A() {std::cout << "~A() called \n";}
69
70     void f() {std::cout << "A::f() called\n";}
```

```
71 };
72
73
74 int main()
75 {
76    auto up = allocate_unique<A>(std::allocator<A>());
77    up->f();
78
79    std::allocator<int> a;
80    auto p = allocate_unique<int>(a, 0);
81    return *p;
82 }
```

It also prints

```
A() called
A::f() called
~A() called
```

0.45   Compile-time integer sequences

*** Question 45   Compile-time integer sequences

Describe the class template provided by the library which can represent an integer sequence at compile time.

Solution of Question 45

That Class template is *std::integer_sequence*, when used as an argument to a function template the parameter pack defining the sequence can be deduced and used in a pack expansion.

```
1 template<class T, T... I>
2 struct integer_sequence
3 {
4      typedef T value_type;
5      static constexpr size_t size() noexcept
6      {
7          return sizeof...(I);
8      }
9 };
```

Note that T is an integer type.

```
1 #include <utility>
2 #include <type_traits>
3
4 // generates empty integer sequence
5 static_assert(std::integer_sequence<int>::size() == 0, "size of std::
     integer_sequence<int> should be zero");
6
7 // generates int : 0, 1, 2, 3, 4, 5
8 static_assert(std::integer_sequence<int, 0, 1, 2, 3, 4, 5>::size() == 6, ""
     );
9
10 static_assert(std::is_same<std::integer_sequence<int>::value_type, int>::
     value, "");
11
12 // generates unsigned short : 3, 8
13 using ushort2 =
14     std::integer_sequence<unsigned short, 3, 8>;
15
16 static_assert(std::is_same<ushort2::value_type, unsigned short>::value, "")
     ;
17 static_assert(ushort2::size() == 2, "");
18
19 static_assert(std::is_same<std::integer_sequence<bool>::value_type, bool>::
     value, "");
```

Alas, the following program gets compiled both with gcc 4.9 and clang 4.5 trunk : both with libstdc++ and libc++ as of this writing:

```
#include <utility>
using float_seq =
    std::integer_sequence<float>;

float_seq::value_type fv;
```

This should fail to compile, since float is not an integral type. I hope that this will be addressed soon in future with incorporating simple code like *static_assert* and *std::is_integral* :

```
 1 template<class T, T... I>
 2 struct integer_sequence
 3 {
 4     typedef T value_type; // or using value_type = T;
 5
 6     static_assert(std::is_integral<T>::value,
 7             "std::integer_sequence can only be instantiated with an
                    integral type");
 8
 9     static constexpr size_t size() noexcept
10     {
11         return sizeof...(I);
12     }
13 };
```

0.46 Simplified Creation of std::integer_sequence

*** Question 46   Simplified Creation of std::integer_sequence

Describe a mechanism to simplify creation of std::integer_sequence.

Solution of Question 46

Fortunately there is an alias template *std::make_integer_sequence* which denotes a specialization of *std::integer_sequence* with N template non-type arguments.

```
template<class T, T N>
using make_integer_sequence =
    std::integer_sequence<T, /* a sequence 0, 1, 2, ..., N-1 */ >;
```

The type *std::make_integer_sequence< T, N >* denotes the type *std::integer_sequence< T, 0, 1, ..., N − 1 >*. *std::make_integer_sequence< int, 0 >* denotes the type *std::integer_sequence< int >*. *std::make_integer_sequence< T, 0 >* denotes the type *std::integer_sequence< T >*.

```
 1 #include <utility>
 2 #include <type_traits>
 3
 4 static_assert(std::is_same<
 5 std::make_integer_sequence<int, 0>,
 6 std::integer_sequence<int>
 7                 >::value,
 8             "make empty int seq");
 9
10 static_assert(std::is_same<
11 std::make_integer_sequence<int, 2>,
12 std::integer_sequence<int, 0, 1>
13                 >::value,
14             "make non-empty int seq");
15
16 static_assert(std::is_same<
17 std::make_integer_sequence<unsigned, 0>,
18 std::integer_sequence<unsigned>
19                 >::value,
20             "make empty unsigned seq");
21
22 static_assert(std::is_same<
23 std::make_integer_sequence<unsigned, 2>,
24 std::integer_sequence<unsigned, 0, 1>
25                 >::value,
```

```
26                    "make non−empty unsigned seq");
27
28 static_assert(std::is_same<
29 std::make_integer_sequence<unsigned long long, 0>,
30 std::integer_sequence<unsigned long long>
31                    >::value, "");
32
33 static_assert(std::is_same<
34 std::make_integer_sequence<unsigned long long, 1>,
35 std::integer_sequence<unsigned long long, 0>
36                    >::value, "");
37
38 static_assert(std::is_same<
39 std::make_integer_sequence<unsigned long long, 2>,
40 std::integer_sequence<unsigned long long, 0, 1>
41                    >::value, "");
42
43 static_assert(std::is_same<
44 std::make_integer_sequence<unsigned long long, 3>,
45 std::integer_sequence<unsigned long long, 0, 1, 2>
46                    >::value, "");
```

Internals

Typical implementation may look like:

```
 1 namespace integer_sequence_internals
 2 {
 3
 4 template <typename T, size_t... Extra>
 5 struct repeat;
 6
 7 template <typename T, T... Is, size_t... Extra>
 8 struct repeat<integer_sequence<T, Is...>, Extra...>
 9 {
10     using type = integer_sequence<T, Is...,
11         1 * sizeof...(Is) + Is...,
12         2 * sizeof...(Is) + Is...,
13         3 * sizeof...(Is) + Is...,
14         4 * sizeof...(Is) + Is...,
15         5 * sizeof...(Is) + Is...,
16         6 * sizeof...(Is) + Is...,
17         7 * sizeof...(Is) + Is...,
18         Extra...>;
19 };
20
21 template <size_t N>
22 struct parity;
23
24 template <size_t N>
25 struct make
26     : parity<N % 8>::template pmake<N> {};
27
28 template <> struct make<0> { using type = integer_sequence<size_t>; };
29 template <> struct make<1> { using type = integer_sequence<size_t, 0>; };
30 template <> struct make<2> { using type = integer_sequence<size_t, 0, 1>;
       };
31 template <> struct make<3> { using type = integer_sequence<size_t, 0, 1,
       2>; };
32 template <> struct make<4> { using type = integer_sequence<size_t, 0, 1, 2,
       3>; };
33 template <> struct make<5> { using type = integer_sequence<size_t, 0, 1, 2,
       3, 4>; };
34 template <> struct make<6> { using type = integer_sequence<size_t, 0, 1, 2,
       3, 4, 5>; };
35 template <> struct make<7> { using type = integer_sequence<size_t, 0, 1, 2,
       3, 4, 5, 6>; };
36
37 template <> struct parity<0> { template <size_t N> struct pmake : repeat<
       typename make<N / 8>::type> {}; };
```

```cpp
38 template <> struct parity<1> { template <size_t N> struct pmake : repeat<
      typename make<N / 8 >::type, N − 1> {}; };
39 template <> struct parity<2> { template <size_t N> struct pmake : repeat<
      typename make<N / 8 >::type, N − 2, N − 1> {}; };
40 template <> struct parity<3> { template <size_t N> struct pmake : repeat<
      typename make<N / 8 >::type, N − 3, N − 2, N − 1> {}; };
41 template <> struct parity<4> { template <size_t N> struct pmake : repeat<
      typename make<N / 8 >::type, N − 4, N − 3, N − 2, N − 1> {}; };
42 template <> struct parity<5> { template <size_t N> struct pmake : repeat<
      typename make<N / 8 >::type, N − 5, N − 4, N − 3, N − 2, N − 1> {}; };
43 template <> struct parity<6> { template <size_t N> struct pmake : repeat<
      typename make<N / 8 >::type, N − 6, N − 5, N − 4, N − 3, N − 2, N − 1>
      {}; };
44 template <> struct parity<7> { template <size_t N> struct pmake : repeat<
      typename make<N / 8 >::type, N − 7, N − 6, N − 5, N − 4, N − 3, N − 2, N
      − 1> {}; };
45
46 template <typename T, typename U>
47 struct convert
48 {
49     template <typename>
50     struct result;
51
52     template <T ... Is>
53     struct result<integer_sequence<T, Is...>>
54     {
55         using type = integer_sequence<U, Is ... >;
56     };
57 };
58
59 template <typename T>
60 struct convert<T, T>
61 {
62     template <typename U>
63     struct result
64     {
65         using type = U;
66     };
67 };
68
69 template <typename T, T N>
70 using make_integer_sequence_unchecked =
71     typename convert<size_t, T>::template result<typename make<N>::type >::
          type;
72
73 template <typename T, T N>
74 struct make_integer_sequence
75 {
76     static_assert(std::is_integral<T>::value,
77         "std::make_integer_sequence can only be instantiated with an
              integral type");
78     static_assert(0 <= N, "std::make_integer_sequence input shall not be
          negative");
79
80     using type = make_integer_sequence_unchecked<T, N>;
81 };
82
83 } // namespace integer_sequence_internals
84
85 template <typename T, T N>
86 using make_integer_sequence = typename integer_sequence_internals::
      make_integer_sequence<T, N>::type;
```

0.47 std::index_sequence

*** Question 47   std::index_sequence

What is *std::index_sequence*?

Solution of Question 47

As we know that the type T should be an integer type (used in the parameter pack) in the class template *std::integer_sequence*. *std::index_sequence* is an alias template, representing *std::integer_sequence* in the case of *std::size_t*:

```cpp
template<std::size_t... I>
using index_sequence =
    std::integer_sequence<std::size_t, I...>;
```

It helps working with the indices of tuples, arrays etc.

```cpp
#include <utility>
#include <type_traits>

// generates size_t : 1, 1, 2, 3, 5
using indices =
    std::index_sequence<1, 1, 2, 3, 5>;

using indices1 =
    std::integer_sequence<std::size_t, 1, 1, 2, 3, 5>;

static_assert(std::is_same<
    indices::value_type,
    std::size_t
>::value, "");

static_assert(indices::size() == 5, "");

static_assert(std::is_same<
    indices,
    indices1
>::value, "");
```

To simplify the creation of *std::index_sequence*, there is a template alias *std::make_index_sequence* :

```cpp
template<std::size_t N>
using make_index_sequence =
    std::make_integer_sequence<std::size_t, N>;
```

```cpp
#include <utility>
#include <type_traits>

static_assert(std::is_same<
std::make_index_sequence<0>,
std::integer_sequence<std::size_t>
                    >::value, "");

static_assert(std::is_same<
std::make_index_sequence<2>,
std::integer_sequence<std::size_t, 0, 1>
                    >::value, "");


static_assert(std::is_same<
std::make_index_sequence<3>,
std::integer_sequence<std::size_t, 0, 1, 2>
                    >::value, "");
```

There is another template alias *std::index_sequence_for* such that *std::index_sequence_for< A, B, C >* is an alias for *std::index_sequence< 0, 1, 2 >*.

```cpp
template<class... T>
using index_sequence_for =
    std::make_index_sequence<sizeof...(T)>;
```

```cpp
#include <utility>
#include <type_traits>

// generates std::size_t : 0, 1, 2, 3
using indices =
    std::index_sequence_for<char, int, std::size_t, unsigned long>;
```

```
 8 static_assert(std::is_same<
 9                indices,
10                std::make_index_sequence<4>
11                >::value, "");
12
13
14 struct A{};
15 struct B{};
16
17 static_assert(std::is_same<
18     std::index_sequence_for<A, B>,
19     std::index_sequence<0, 1>
20 >::value, "");
```

0.48 Custom Sequence : Addition

*** Question 48   Custom Sequence : Addition

Generate a custom sequence by addition of a constant to all the elements of a given integer sequence, i.e.

std::integer_sequence<T, I...>

gets transformed to

std::integer_sequence<T, N+I...>

for a compile time constant N.

Solution of Question 48

```
 1 #include <utility>
 2
 3 template<int N, typename T, T... I>
 4 constexpr std::integer_sequence<T, N+I...>
 5 add(std::integer_sequence<T, I...>) noexcept
 6 {
 7     return {};
 8 }
 9
10 using orig_seq =
11     std::integer_sequence<std::size_t, 1, 2, 3, 4, 5>;
12
13 using expected_seq =
14     std::integer_sequence<std::size_t, 6, 7, 8, 9, 10>;
15
16 auto add5_seq = add<5>(orig_seq());
17
18 static_assert(std::is_same<decltype(add5_seq), expected_seq>::value, "");
```

0.49 Custom Sequence : Multiply

*** Question 49   Custom Sequence : Multiply

Generate a custom sequence by multiplication by a constant to all the elements of a given integer sequence, i.e.

std::integer_sequence<T, I...>

gets transformed to

std::integer_sequence<T, N * I...>

for a compile time constant N.

Solution of Question 49

```
1 #include <utility>
2
3 template<int N, typename T, T... I>
4 constexpr std::integer_sequence<T, N*I...>
5 multiply(std::integer_sequence<T, I...>) noexcept
6 {
7     return {};
8 }
9
10 using orig_seq =
11     std::integer_sequence<std::size_t, 1, 2, 3, 4, 5>;
12
13 using expected_seq =
14     std::integer_sequence<std::size_t, 5, 10, 15, 20, 25>;
15
16 auto mult5_seq = multiply<5>(orig_seq());
17
18 static_assert(std::is_same<decltype(mult5_seq), expected_seq>::value, "");
```

0.50 Custom Sequence : Split

*** Question 50   Custom Sequence : Split

Generate two custom sequences by splitting a given integer sequence such that

std::integer_sequence<T, I0, I... >

gets transformed to

std::integer_sequence<T, I0>

and

std::integer_sequence<T, I... >

Solution of Question 50

```
1 #include <utility>
2
3 template<typename T, T I0, T... I>
4 constexpr std::integer_sequence<T, I0>
5 split1(std::integer_sequence<T, I0, I...>) noexcept
6 {
7     return {};
8 }
9
10
11 template<typename T, T I0, T... I>
12 constexpr std::integer_sequence<T, I...>
13 split2(std::integer_sequence<T, I0, I...>) noexcept
14 {
15     return {};
16 }
17
18
19 using orig_seq =
20     std::integer_sequence<std::size_t, 1, 2, 3, 4, 5>;
21
22 using expected_seq1 =
23     std::integer_sequence<std::size_t, 1>;
24
25 using expected_seq2 =
26     std::integer_sequence<std::size_t, 2, 3, 4, 5>;
27
28 auto seq1 = split1(orig_seq());
29 auto seq2 = split2(orig_seq());
30
31 static_assert(std::is_same<decltype(seq1), expected_seq1>::value, "");
32 static_assert(std::is_same<decltype(seq2), expected_seq2>::value, "");
```

0.51 Extract from tuple

*** Question 51   Extract from tuple

Develop an utility to help extract the elements of the tuple against a given sequence of tuple's indices.

Solution of Question 51

```
1 #include <tuple>
2 #include <utility>
3 #include <type_traits>
4 #include <cassert>
5
6
7 template <typename Container, typename T, T... I>
8 auto extract ( const Container &t, const std::integer_sequence<T, I...> idx
       )
9       -> decltype ( std::make_tuple ( std::get<I>(t)... ))
10 {
11      return  std::make_tuple ( std::get<I>(t)... );
12 }
13
14
15 int main()
16 {
17 //  Make a couple of sequences
18      using int3    = std::make_integer_sequence<int, 3>;      // generates
          int:    0,1,2
19      using size7   = std::make_integer_sequence<size_t, 7>;  // generates
          size_t: 0,1,2,3,4,5,6
20      using size4   = std::make_index_sequence<4>;      // generates
          size_t: 0,1,2,3
21      using size2   = std::index_sequence_for<int, size_t>;  // generates
          size_t: 0,1
22      using intmix  = std::integer_sequence<int, 9, 8, 7, 2>; // generates
          int:    9,8,7,2
23      using sizemix = std::index_sequence<1, 1, 2, 3, 5>;      // generates
          size_t: 1,1,2,3,5
24
25 //  Make sure they're what we expect
26      static_assert ( std::is_same<int3::value_type, int>::value, "int3 type
          wrong" );
27      static_assert ( int3::size () == 3, "int3 size wrong" );
28
29      static_assert ( std::is_same<size7::value_type, size_t>::value, "size7
          type wrong" );
30      static_assert ( size7::size () == 7, "size7 size wrong" );
31
32      static_assert ( std::is_same<size4::value_type, size_t>::value, "size4
          type wrong" );
33      static_assert ( size4::size () == 4, "size4 size wrong" );
34
35      static_assert ( std::is_same<size2::value_type, size_t>::value, "size2
          type wrong" );
36      static_assert ( size2::size () == 2, "size2 size wrong" );
37
38      static_assert ( std::is_same<intmix::value_type, int>::value, "intmix
          type wrong" );
39      static_assert ( intmix::size () == 4, "intmix size wrong" );
40
41      static_assert ( std::is_same<sizemix::value_type, size_t>::value, "
          sizemix type wrong" );
42      static_assert ( sizemix::size () == 5, "sizemix size wrong" );
43
44      auto tup = std::make_tuple ( 10, 11, 12, 13, 14, 15, 16, 17, 18, 19, 20
          );
45
46 //  Use them
47      auto t3 = extract ( tup, int3() );
```

```
48    static_assert ( std::tuple_size<decltype(t3)>::value == int3::size (),
          "t3 size wrong");
49    assert ( t3 == std::make_tuple ( 10, 11, 12 ));
50
51    auto t7 = extract ( tup, size7 ());
52    static_assert ( std::tuple_size<decltype(t7)>::value == size7::size (),
          "t7 size wrong");
53    assert ( t7 == std::make_tuple ( 10, 11, 12, 13, 14, 15, 16 ));
54
55    auto t4 = extract ( tup, size4 ());
56    static_assert ( std::tuple_size<decltype(t4)>::value == size4::size (),
          "t4 size wrong");
57    assert ( t4 == std::make_tuple ( 10, 11, 12, 13 ));
58
59    auto t2 = extract ( tup, size2 ());
60    static_assert ( std::tuple_size<decltype(t2)>::value == size2::size (),
          "t2 size wrong");
61    assert ( t2 == std::make_tuple ( 10, 11 ));
62
63    auto tintmix = extract ( tup, intmix ());
64    static_assert ( std::tuple_size<decltype(tintmix)>::value == intmix::
          size (), "tintmix size wrong");
65    assert ( tintmix == std::make_tuple ( 19, 18, 17, 12 ));
66
67    auto tsizemix = extract ( tup, sizemix ());
68    static_assert ( std::tuple_size<decltype(tsizemix)>::value == sizemix::
          size (), "tsizemix size wrong");
69    assert ( tsizemix == std::make_tuple ( 11, 11, 12, 13, 15 ));
70 }
```

0.52   convert *std::array* to *std::tuple*

*** Question 52   convert *std::array* to *std::tuple*

Write a program to convert *std::array* to *std::tuple*.

Solution of Question 52

```
1 #include <utility>
2 #include <tuple>
3 #include <array>
4 #include <cassert>
5
6 template<typename Array, size_t... I>
7 auto array_to_tuple_(const Array& a, std::index_sequence<I...>)
8     -> decltype(std::make_tuple(a[I]...))
9 {
10    return std::make_tuple(a[I]...);
11 }
12
13
14 template<typename T, std::size_t N, typename Indices = std::
        make_index_sequence<N>>
15 auto array_to_tuple(const std::array<T, N>& a)
16     -> decltype(array_to_tuple_(a, Indices()))
17 {
18    return array_to_tuple_(a, Indices());
19 }
20
21
22 int main()
23 {
24    std::array<int, 5> a = {1, 2, 3, 4, 5};
25
26    auto t = array_to_tuple(a);
27
28    auto t1 = std::make_tuple(1, 2, 3, 4, 5);
29
30    assert(t == t1);
```

31 }

0.53   Piecewise construction of std::pair

*** Question 53   Piecewise construction of std::pair

Explain how piecewise construction of std::pair works.

Solution of Question 53

The *struct piecewise_construct_t* is an empty structure type used as a unique type to disambiguate constructor and function overloading.

```
struct piecewise_construct_t { };
constexpr piecewise_construct_t piecewise_construct = piecewise_construct_t
    ();
```

Specifically, *pair* has a constructor with *piecewise_construct_t* as the first argument, immediately followed by two tuple arguments used for piecewise construction of the elements of the pair object:

```
template <class... Args1, class... Args2>
pair(piecewise_construct_t,
tuple<Args1...> first_args, tuple<Args2...> second_args);
```

The constructor initializes first with arguments of types *Args1...* obtained by forwarding the elements of *first_args* and initializes second with arguments of types *Args2...* obtained by forwarding the elements of *second_args*.

Note that, forwarding an element x of type U within a tuple object means calling

```
std::forward<U>(x).
```

This form of construction, whereby constructor arguments for first and second are each provided in a separate tuple object, is called *piecewise construction*.

One implementation technique is to delegate to a private constructor for *pair* that takes two types like *std::index_sequence*:

```
template<class... Args1, class... Args2>
pair(std::piecewise_construct_t, std::tuple<Args1...> args1, std::tuple<
    Args2...> args2)
    :
std::pair(args1, args2, std::index_sequence_for<Args1...>{}, std::
    index_sequence_for<Args2...>{})
{ }

private:

template<class... A1, class... A2, size_t... I1, size_t... I2>
pair(std::tuple<A1...>& a1, std::tuple<A2...>& a2, std::index_sequence<I1
    ...>, std::index_sequence<I2...>)
    :
first(std::get<I1>(std::move(a1))...),
second(std::get<I2>(std::move(a2))...)
{ }
```

0.54   Compile Time Integer Sequence Simplified

*** Question 54   Compile Time Integer Sequence Simplified

Provide a simplified implementation sketch of the integer sequences discussed so far.

Solution of Question 54

```
1 #include <cstddef>
2 #include <type_traits>
3
4 // A type that represents a parameter pack of zero or more integers.
5 template<typename T, T... I>
```

```
 6 struct integer_sequence
 7 {
 8     static_assert ( std :: is_integral<T>:: value , "Integral type" );
 9
10     using type = T;
11
12     static constexpr T size = sizeof ...(I);
13
14     // Generate an integer_sequence with an additional element.
15     template<T N>
16         using append = integer_sequence<T, I ... , N>;
17
18     using next = append<size >;
19 };
20
21 template<typename T, T ... I>
22 constexpr T integer_sequence<T, I ... >:: size ;
23
24 template<std :: size_t ... I>
25     using index_sequence =
26         integer_sequence<std :: size_t , I ... >;
27
28
29 // Metafunction that generates an integer_sequence of T containing [0, N)
30 template<typename T, T Nt, std :: size_t N>
31 struct iota
32 {
33     static_assert ( Nt >= 0, "N cannot be negative" );
34
35     using type =
36         typename iota<T, Nt−1, N−1>:: type :: next ;
37 };
38
39 // Terminal case of the recursive metafunction.
40 template<typename T, T Nt>
41 struct iota<T, Nt, 0ul>
42 {
43     using type = integer_sequence<T>;
44 };
45
46
47 // make_integer_sequence<T, N> is an alias for integer_sequence<T, 0 ,...N
          −1>
48 template<typename T, T N>
49     using make_integer_sequence =
50         typename iota<T, N, N>:: type ;
51
52 // make_index_sequence<N> is an alias for make_integer_sequence<std :: size_t
          , N>
53 template<int N>
54     using make_index_sequence =
55         make_integer_sequence<std :: size_t , N>;
56
57
58 // index_sequence_for<A, B, C> is an alias for index_sequence <0, 1, 2>
59 template<typename ... Args>
60     using index_sequence_for =
61         make_index_sequence<sizeof ...( Args)>;
```

0.55   sfinae and represent type of function

*** Question 55   sfinae and represent type of function

Develop a generic function object *increment_me* for incrementing the passed-in values of incrementable types so that the following call will print 6:

```
std :: cout << increment_me ()(5) << std :: endl;
```

Illustrate how it can be used as a normal function *call_increment_me* like :

```
std :: cout << call_increment_me (5) << std :: endl;
```

Also keep into account to let it call another function with same name to be used with non incrementable types without any compiler error.

Solution of Question 55

```
struct increment_me
{
    template<typename T>
    auto operator()(T t) const
        -> decltype(++t)
    {
        return ++t;
    }
};
```

```
template <typename T>
typename std::result_of<increment_me(T)>::type
call_increment_me(T t)
{
    return increment_me()(t);
}
```

std::result_of is essentially a *metafunction* to return the type of an expression.
Alternatively, we can rewrite the above function as:

```
template <typename T>
decltype(std::declval<increment_me>()(std::declval<T>()))
call_increment_me(T t)
{
    return increment_me()(t);
}
```

Now if we try to use this function with non incrementable types like *std::string*, then this result into compiler error citing substitution failure.

We would like to enjoy the fact that in C++14, *std::result_of* is *SFINAE* friendly.

```
template <typename T>
typename std::result_of<increment_me(T)>::type
call_increment_me(T t)
{
    return increment_me()(t);
}


struct A {};
struct B { template<typename T> B(T const &) {} };

A call_increment_me(B)
{
    std::cout << "A call_increment_me() called" << std::endl;
    return A();
}
```

So, the following client code :

```
std::cout << increment_me()(5) << std::endl;
std::cout << call_increment_me(5) << std::endl;
call_increment_me(std::string("5"));
```

will print :

```
6
6
A call_increment_me() called
```

Please note that in pre-C++14 era, *std::result_of* was not sfinae friendly, resulting into a hard error. So user had no choice other than to rely on *decl* variant which is a bit mouthful in this case.

0.56   metafunction : check presence of type member

**** Question 56   metafunction : check presence of type member

Develop an utility in a form of trait-like metafunction to determine whether a type T has a type member named *type*.

Solution of Question 56

```
1 #include <type_traits>
2 #include <iomanip>
3 #include <iostream>
4
5 template< class T >
6     using void_t = void;
7     //using void_t = std::conditional_t<true, void, T>;
8
9
10 template< class , class = void >
11 struct has_type_member : std::false_type
12 { };
13
14 template< class T >
15 struct has_type_member<T, void_t<typename T::type>> : std::true_type
16 { };
17
18 struct A
19 {
20     typedef int type;
21 };
22
23 struct B
24 {
25 };
26
27 int main()
28 {
29     static_assert(has_type_member<A>::value, "");
30     static_assert(!has_type_member<B>::value, "");
31
32     std::cout << std::boolalpha;
33     std::cout << has_type_member<A>() << std::endl;
34     std::cout << has_type_member<B>() << std::endl;
35     std::cout << has_type_member< std::common_type<int, double> >{}() <<
              std::endl;
36     std::cout << has_type_member< std::common_type<int, std::string> >{}()
              << std::endl;
37
38 }
```

It prints :

```
true
false
true
false
```

Compared to traditional code that computes such a result, this version seems considerably simpler, and has no special cases (e.g., to avoid forming any pointer-to-reference type).

The purpose of the *void_t* alias template is simply to map any given type to *void*.

On some platforms, it may issue error citing unused argument T in the alias template specialization, so we may need to use the following code instead:

```
using void_t = std::conditional_t<true, void, T>;
```

conditional_t works as a workaround to ensure that our template's argument is always used.

The code features exactly two cases, each straightforward:

1. when there is a type member named *type*, the specialization is well-formed (with *void* as its second argument) and will be selected, producing a *true_type* result

2. when there is no such type member, *SFINAE* will apply, the specialization will be nonviable, and the primary template will be selected instead, yielding *false_type*.

Thus, each case obtains the appropriate result.

Kindly note that we can extend the code for *void_t* to be used for mapping a sequence of types to *void*.

```
1 template< class ... >
2 struct voider { using type = void; };
3
4 template< class ... T0toN >
5 using void_t = = typename voider<T0toN... >::type;
```

0.57 std::common_type and sfinae

**** Question 57   std::common_type and sfinae

Provide a suitable implementation of *common_type* trait so as to avoid a hard error when there is no common type, and thus to make the trait conveniently usable in a SFINAE context.

Solution of Question 57

First let us develop an alias template, which encapsulates the basic mechanism for determining the type, if any, common to two given types T and U:

```
template< class T, class U >
    using common_type_helper =
        decltype(declval<bool>() ? declval<T>() : declval<U>());
```

A specialization of the *common_type_helper* template is ill-formed whenever its conditional expression is ill-formed, i.e., when T and U have no type in common.

Let us develop another helper class to handle all cases where there is no common type, for example, in a given list of types, there could be two adjacent types such that

- neither can be converted to any form of the other, or
- there is no third type to which both can be converted.

This case also arises when the given list of types is empty.

```
template< class, class ... >
struct ctype { };
```

Let us specialize this template to handle the case of a single type:

```
template< class T >
struct ctype<void,T>
{
    using type = decay_t<T>;
};
```

The second specialization handles the general case of two or more types:

```
template< class T, class U, class ... V >
struct ctype<void_t<common_type_helper<T,U>>, T, U, V... >
:
ctype<void, common_type_helper<T,U>, V... > { };
```

This specialization will be viable only so long as the first two types in the argument list of types have a common type as defined by *common_type_helper*.

If the first two types have no common type, both specializations will be nonviable and so the primary template will be selected to terminate the recursion. Otherwise, once the list has been recursively pairwise reduced to a single type, the first specialization will be selected.

```
template <class ... T>
struct common_type : ctype<void, T... > {};
```

- If *sizeof...(T)* is zero, there shall be no member *type*.
- If *sizeof...(T)* is one, let *T0* denote the sole type comprising *T*. The member typedef *type* shall denote the same type as

    decay_t<T0>

- If *sizeof...(T)* is greater than one, let *T*1, *T*2, and *R* respectively denote the first, second, and (pack of) remaining types comprising *T*. *sizeof...(R)* may be zero. Finally, let *C* denote the type, if any, of an unevaluated conditional expression whose first operand is an arbitrary value of type *bool*, whose second operand is an *xvalue* of type *T*1, and whose third operand is an *xvalue* of type *T*2. If there is such a type *C*, the member typedef *type* shall denote the same type, if any, as

common_type_t<C,R...>

Otherwise, there shall be no member *type*.

0.58 Contextual Conversion

*** Question 58   Contextual Conversion

Implement a class template that wraps a value of arithmetic or pointer type *T*, ensuring that the wrapped value will by default be initialized with *T*'s zero value.

Demonstrate its use in contexts like deletion of a pointer to a dynamic instance of this class and switch-case scenarios with integer instances.

Solution of Question 58

Simple design of the desired class is:

Program 2: class template : wrapper for arithmetic or pointer types

```
1 #include <cassert>
2 #include <type_traits>
3
4 template<
5     class T,
6     class = typename
7              std::enable_if<
8                        std::is_arithmetic<T>::value
9                     || std::is_pointer<T>::value
10               >::type
11 >
12 struct zero_init
13 {
14     zero_init( )
15     : val( static_cast<T>(0) )
16     { }
17
18     zero_init( T val ) : val( val )
19     { }
20
21     operator T & ( )
22     { return val; }
23
24     operator T( ) const
25     { return val; }
26
27 private:
28     T val;
29 };
```

Please note that two conversion operators are provided to cover the case of *const* and *non-const* objects being treated differently.

Simplified usage looks like:

Program 3: conversion with pointer and value

```
1 int main()
2 {
3     zero_init<int*> p;
4     assert( p == 0 );
5
6     p = new int(7);
7     assert( *p == 7 );
8
```

```
 9        delete p;
10
11        zero_init<int> i;  assert( i == 0 );
12        i = 7;
13        assert( i == 7 );
14
15        switch( i )
16        {
17            case 7 :
18            std::cout << "7" << std::endl;
19            default :
20            exit(0);
21        }
22 }
```

It simply prints: 7.

Caveat : Certain compilers, which are not C++14 complaint, may lead to the following scenarios:

- *delete p* may produce diagnostics.
- the expression *i* in *switch* may be ill-formed.

The issue here is because of the restriction being implied by *single non-explicit conversion function* with pre-c++14. And certain contextual conversion rules that limit a class to only one conversion operator while allowing for the conversion of a value of the class's type to a corresponding value of a type specified by the context.

Workaround with pre-C++14 Compilers : To address these embarrassing situations, simple workarounds may be to use *delete (p+0)* or *delete +p* instead of *delete p*.

Similarly, we may use *switch(i + 0)* or *switch(+i)* instead of *switch(i)*.

Going forward, C++14 lifted these restrictions on contextual conversions by supporting the proven approach of contextually conversion to *bool*. This change avoids the need for the embarrassing workarounds shown above as well as it brings the benefit of more consistent behavior by eliminating the special cases for contextual conversions, aligning them with the rules for the C++11 contextual conversion to *bool*.

0.59 Single quotation mark as digit separator

** Question 59   Single quotation mark as digit separator

What is the output of the following program ?

Program 4: Single quotation mark as digit separator

```
 1 #include <iostream>
 2
 3 #define M(x, ...) __VA_ARGS__
 4
 5 int main()
 6 {
 7     /*auto million = 1'000'000;
 8     auto pi = 3.14159'26535'89793;
 9
10     std::cout << "million is : " << million << std::endl;
11     std::cout << "pi is : " << pi << std::endl;*/
12
13     int x[2] = { M(1'2,3'4) };
14
15     for(auto e : x)
16     std::cout << e << std::endl;
17 }
```

Solution of Question 59

The code does get compiled with C++11, because the single quotes delimit a character literal in C++2011.

The error with clang++ 3.5

clang++ -std=c++11 digit_separator.cpp is:

```
digit_separator.cpp:7:21:
error: expected ';' at end of declaration
    auto million = 1'000'000;
                    ^
                    ;
digit_separator.cpp:8:22:
error: expected ';' at end of declaration
    auto pi = 3.14159'26535'89793;
                     ^
                     ;
2 errors generated.
```

Let us get rid of the lines containing these errors, then C++11 compilers compiles it fine and but the output is

```
0
0
```

Whereas with C++14 compilers,
clang++ -std=c++1y digit_separator.cpp, it correctly prints the values of *million* and *pi* and the array *x* is

```
34
0
```

Because because the single quotes are digit separators in C++14. Hence the single-quote character ' can now be used anywhere within a numeric literal for aesthetic readability. It does not affect the numeric value.

Similarly, the float literals $1.602'176'565e - 19$ and $1.602176565e - 19$ have the same value. Optional separating single quotes in a digit-sequence are ignored when determining its value.

Along the same lines :
the literals 10485764, $1'048'576$, $0X100000$, $0x10'0000$, and $0'004'000'000$ all have the same value.

0.60 Binary Literals

** Question 60   Binary literals

What is a *Binary Literal* ?

Solution of Question 60

A binary integer literal (base two) begins with 0b or 0B and consists of a sequence of binary digits.

Integer constants can be written as binary constants, consisting of a sequence of '0' and '1' digits, prefixed by '0b' or '0B'. This is particularly useful in environments that operate a lot on the bit level (like microcontrollers).

The following statements are identical:

```
1      i =        42;
2      i =      0x2a;
3      i =       052;
4      i = 0b101010;
```

The type of these constants follows the same rules as for octal or hexadecimal integer constants, so suffixes like 'L' or 'UL' can be applied.

Integers can be specified in decimal, binary, octal, or hexadecimal.

Decimal integers are a sequence of decimal digits.

Binary integers are a sequence of binary digits preceded by a '0b'.

Octal integers are a sequence of octal digits preceded by a '0'.

Hexadecimal integers are a sequence of hexadecimal digits preceded by a '0x'.

Integers can have embedded '_' characters, which are ignored. The embedded '_' are useful for formatting long literals, such as using them as a thousands separator:

```
1 123_456      // 123456
2 1_2_3_4_5_6_  // 123456
```

The number *twelve* can be represented as :

Program 5: representation of *twelve*

```
1 #include <cassert>
2
3 int main()
4 {
5     auto x1 = 12;   // decimal
6     auto x2 = 014;  // octal
7     auto x3 = 0XC;  // hexadecimal
8     auto x4 = 0b1100;  // binary
9     auto x5 = 0B1100;  // binary
10
11    assert(x1 == x2);
12    assert(x2 == x3);
13    assert(x3 == x4);
14    assert(x4 == x5);
15 }
```

0.61 *auto* return type in function declaration

*** Question 61   auto return type in function declaration

Review the code fragments below:

```
1 struct A
2 {
3     auto f();
4 };
5 auto A::f() { return 42; }
```

```
1 auto f();
2 auto f() { return 42; }
3 auto f();
4 int  f();
```

```
1 template <class T> auto g(T t);
2 template <class T> auto g(T t) { return t; }
3 template <class T> auto g(T t);
```

```
1 auto f();
2 int i = f();
```

```
1 template <class T> auto f(T t) { return t; }
2 template auto f(int);
3 template char f(char);
4 template<> auto f(double);
5
6 template <class T> T f(T t) { return t; }
7 template char f(char);
8 template auto f(float);
```

Solution of Question 61

Allowing non-defining function declarations with auto return type is not strictly necessary, but it is useful for coding styles that prefer to define member functions outside the class:

```
1 struct A
2 {
3     auto f(); // forward declaration
4 };
5 auto A::f() { return 42; }
```

Non-defining declarations are allowed so long as all declarations have the same declared type, without considering the deduced type.

```
1 auto f(); // return type is unknown
2 auto f() { return 42; } // return type is int
3 auto f(); // redeclaration
4 int  f(); // error, declares a different function
```

Similar rules apply for function templates as well:

```
1 template <class T> auto g(T t); // forward declaration
2 template <class T> auto g(T t) { return t; } // return type is deduced at
      instantiation time
3 template <class T> auto g(T t); // redeclaration
```

Using such a function in an expression when only a forward declaration has been seen is ill-formed:

```
1 auto f();      // return type is unknown
2 int i = f(); // error, return type of f is unknown
```

An explicit specialization or instantiation of an auto template must also use auto. An explicit specialization or instantiation of a non-auto template must not use auto.

```
1 template <class T> auto f(T t) { return t; } // #1
2 template auto f(int); // OK
3 template char f(char); // error, no matching template
4 template<> auto f(double); // OK, forward declaration with unknown return
      type
5
6 template <class T> T f(T t) { return t; } // OK, not functionally
      equivalent to #1
7 template char f(char); // OK, now there is a matching template
8 template auto f(float); // OK, matches #1
```

0.62   return type deduction for function

*** Question 62   return type deduction for function

Is the following code valid ?

Program 6: return type deduction for function
```
1 auto iterate(int len)
2 {
3   for (int i = 0; i < len; ++i)
4     if (i == 10)
5       return i;
6   return −1;
7 }
8
9 int main()
10 {
11    iterate(15);
12 }
```

Solution of Question 62

No in C++11. The typical error may be :

```
multiple_return.cpp:1:1:
error: 'auto' return without trailing return type;
      deduced return types are a C++1y extension
auto iterate(int len)
^

1 error generated.
```

In C++11, there is limitation on return type deduction to function bodies consisting of a single return statement.

But it is valid in C++14.

Both return statements here return *int*, we can determine that perfectly well.

If a function with a declared return type that contains a placeholder type *auto* has multiple return statements, the return type is deduced for each return statement. In either case, if the type deduced is not the same in each deduction, the program is ill-formed.

If a function with a declared return type that uses a placeholder type has no return statements, the return type is deduced as though from a return statement with no operand at the closing brace of the function body.

```
1 auto   f() { }  // OK, return type is void
2 auto*  g() { }  // error, cannot deduce auto* from void()
```

If the type of an entity with an undeduced placeholder type is needed to determine the type of an expression, the program is ill-formed. But once a return statement has been seen in a function, the return type deduced from that statement can be used in the rest of the function, including in other return statements.

```
1     auto n = n;  // error, n's type is unknown
2     auto f();
3     void g() { &f; }  // error, f's return type is unknown
4     auto sum(int i) {
5        if (i == 1)
6           return i;  // sum's return type is int
7        else
8           return sum(i−1)+i;  // OK, sum's return type has been deduced
9     }
```

0.63   return type deduction for lambdas

*** Question 63   return type deduction for lambdas

Is the following code valid ? If yes, what is the return type of the lambda.

Program 7: return type deduction for lambdas

```
1 struct A
2 {
3     int  f();
4     const int& g();
5 };
6
7 template <class T>
8 void h ()
9 {
10     [](T t, bool b)
11     {
12        if (b)
13           return t.f();
14        else
15           return t.g();
16     };
17 }
18
19 template void h<A>();
```

Solution of Question 63

Yes, it is a legal code and lambda return type is *int*.

The restriction, that the return type of a lambda can be deduced only if the body of the lambda consists of a single return statement, has been uplifted.

In particular, multiple return statements could be permitted if they all return the same type.

0.64   return type deduction for lambdas contd..

**** Question 64   return type deduction for lambda

What are the return types of the following lambdas?

Program 8: return type deduction for lambda

```
1 auto x1 = [](int i){ return i; };
2 auto x2 = []{ return { 1, 2 }; };
3
4 int j;
5 auto x3 = []()->auto&& { return j; };
```

Solution of Question 64

clang++ 3.5 gives the following error:

```
lambda_return1.cpp:2:22:
error: cannot deduce lambda return type from
    initializer list
auto x2 = []{ return { 1, 2 }; };
                     ^~~~~~~~

1 error generated.
```

The lambda return type is *auto*, which is replaced by the *trailing-return-type* if provided and/or deduced from return statements.

Thus, *auto* is allowed in *trailing-return-type* because there is the only way to specify that a lambda returns by a deduced reference type:

```
1 []()->auto& { return f(); }
```

For *x*1, return type is *int*.
For *x*3, return type is *int&*.

Deduction from an initializer-list is prohibited. Although a variable declared *auto* and initialized with a brace-enclosed initializer list gets a type of *std::initializer_list*, it is not allowed for a function return type because the underlying array is allocated on the stack, it would immediately leak on return, and any use of the return value would have undefined behavior.

0.65   decltype(auto)

**** Question 65   decltype(auto)

What is *decltype(auto)* ?

Solution of Question 65

For an expression *e*, The type denoted by *decltype(e)* is defined as follows:

- if *e* is an unparenthesized id-expression or an unparenthesized class member access, *decltype(e)* is the type of the entity named by *e*. If there is no such entity, or if *e* names a set of overloaded functions, the program is ill-formed;
- otherwise, if *e* is an *xvalue*, *decltype(e)* is *T&&*, where *T* is the type of *e*;
- otherwise, if *e* is an *lvalue*, *decltype(e)* is *T&*, where *T* is the type of *e*;
- otherwise, *decltype(e)* is the type of *e*.

```
1 const int&& foo();
2 int i;
3 struct A { double x; };
4 const A* a = new A();
5 decltype(foo()) x1 = i;    // type is const int&&
6 decltype(i) x2;            // type is int
7 decltype(a->x) x3;         // type is double
8 decltype((a->x)) x4 = x3;  // type is const double&
```

The auto and decltype(auto) type-specifiers designate a placeholder type that will be replaced later, either by deduction from an initializer or by explicit specification with a trailing-return-type. If the function declarator includes a trailing-return-type, that specifies the declared return type of the function. If the declared return type of the function contains a placeholder type, the return type of the function is deduced from return statements in the body of the function, if any.

The type of a variable declared using auto or decltype(auto) is deduced from its initializer. This use is allowed when declaring variables in a block, in namespace scope, and in a for-init-statement.

```
1 auto x = 5;              // OK: x has type int
2 const auto *v = &x, u = 6;  // OK: v has type const int*, u has type const
      int
3 static auto y = 0.0;      // OK: y has type double
4 auto int r;               // error: auto is not a storage-class-specifier
5 auto f() -> int;          // OK: f returns int
6 auto g() { return 0.0; }  // OK: g returns double
7 auto h();                 // OK, h's return type will be deduced when it
      is defined
8
9 auto x1 = { 1, 2 };       // decltype(x1) is std::initializer_list<int>
10 auto x2 = { 1, 2.0 };    // error: cannot deduce element type
```

If the placeholder is the decltype(auto) type-specifier, the declared type of the variable or return type of the function shall be the placeholder alone:

```
1 int i;
2 int&& f();
3 auto          x3a = i;     // decltype(x3a) is int
4 decltype(auto) x3d = i;    // decltype(x3d) is int
5 auto          x4a = (i);   // decltype(x4a) is int
6 decltype(auto) x4d = (i);  // decltype(x4d) is int&
7 auto          x5a = f();   // decltype(x5a) is int
8 decltype(auto) x5d = f();  // decltype(x5d) is int&&
9 auto          x6a = { 1, 2 }; // decltype(x6a) is std::initializer_list<
      int>
10 decltype(auto) x6d = { 1, 2 }; // error, { 1, 2 } is not an expression
11 auto          *x7a = &i;   // decltype(x7a) is int*
12 decltype(auto)*x7d = &i;   // error, declared type is not plain
      decltype(auto)
```

0.66 return type deduction for function templates

*** Question 66   return type deduction for function templates

What is the rule of deduction for return types in case of function templates with a placeholder ?

Solution of Question 66

Return type deduction for a function template with a placeholder in its declared type occurs when the definition is instantiated even if the function body contains a return statement with a non-type-dependent operand.

So any use of a specialization of the function template will cause an implicit instantiation. Any errors that arise from this instantiation are not in the immediate context of the function type, and can result in the program being ill-formed.

```
1  template <class T> auto f(T t) { return t; } // return type deduced at
       instantiation time
2  typedef decltype(f(1)) fint_t; // instantiates f<int> to deduce return
       type
3  template<class T> auto f(T* t) { return *t; }
4  void g() { int (*p)(int*) = &f; } // instantiates both 'f's to
       determine return types, chooses second
```

Redeclarations or specializations of a function or function template with a declared return type that uses a placeholder type shall also use that placeholder, not a deduced type.

```
1    auto  f();
2    auto  f()  { return  42; }  // return  type  is  int
3    auto  f();  // OK
4    int  f();   // error,  cannot  be  overloaded  with  auto  f()
5    decltype(auto)  f();  // error,  auto  and  decltype(auto)  don't  match
6
7    template <typename T> auto  g(T t)  { return  t; }  // #1
8    template auto  g(int);       // OK,  return  type  is  int
9    template char  g(char);      // error,  no  matching  template
10   template<> auto  g(double);  // OK,  forward  declaration  with  unknown
                return  type
11
12   template <class T> T  g(T t)  { return  t; }  // OK,  not  functionally
              equivalent  to  #1
13   template char  g(char);      // OK,  now  there  is  a  matching  template
14   template auto  g(float);     // still  matches  #1
15
16   void  h()  { return  g(42); }  // error,  ambiguous
17
18   template <typename T> struct  A {
19     friend  T  frf(T);
20   };
21   auto  frf(int  i)  { return  i; }  // not  a  friend  of  A<int>
```

0.67   explicit instantiation and auto

*** Question 67   explicit instantiation and auto

Review the code below:

```
1 template <typename T> auto  f(T t)  { return  t; }
2 extern template auto  f(int);
3 int  (*p)(int) = f;
```

Solution of Question 67

An explicit instantiation declaration does not cause the instantiation of an entity declared using a placeholder type, but it also does not prevent that entity from being instantiated as needed to determine its type.

Hence the line below does not instantiate $f < int >$.

```
1 extern template auto  f(int);
```

Whereas the next line instantiates $f < int >$ to determine its return type, but an explicit instantiation definition is still required somewhere in the program:

```
1 int  (*p)(int) = f;
```

Like constexpr functions, it can be necessary to instantiate an auto function template even if it is not odr-used.

```
1 template <class T> auto  f(T t)  { return  t; }  // return  type  deduced  at
              instantiation  time
2 typedef decltype(f(1))  fint_t;  // must  instantiate  f<int>  to  deduce  return
       type
```

Kindly note that as far as *SFINAE* is concerned, since the return type is deduced by instantiating the template, if the instantiation is ill-formed, this causes an error rather than a substitution failure. This allows an *auto* function to return a lambda, which is not possible using the *decltype(returned expression)* pattern.

The declarator of a variable declared with auto is not limited in the form of the declarator; the same should be true of a function with deduced return type. In particular, this is the only way to deduce return by reference:

```
1    template <class T> struct  A { static  T t; };
2    template <class T> auto&  f()  { return  A::t; }  // returns  by  reference
```

To allow this, we should use the same auto deduction rules for function and lambda return type that we do for auto variables.

Such a function must have a return statement, however, since there is no way to get *void* from *auto&*.

```
1    auto& f() { } // error, no return statement
```

0.68 return type deduction and virtual

** Question 68   return type deduction and virtual

How return type deduction works with virtual functions ?

Solution of Question 68

A function declared with a return type that uses a placeholder type cannot be virtual.

It would be possible to allow return type deduction for virtual functions, but that would complicate both override checking and vtable layout, so it seems preferable to prohibit this.

As a side note, study the illegal code below:

```
1 auto h() { return h(); } // error, return type of h is unknown
```

0.69 deduce return type

** Question 69   deduce return type

What are the return types of the following functions *f1* and *g1*?

```
1 std::string  f();
2 std::string&  g();
3
4 decltype(auto)  f1()
5 {
6     auto str = f();
7     return str;
8 }
9
10 decltype(auto)  g1()
11 {
12     auto str = g();
13     return(str);
14 }
```

Solution of Question 69

f1 returns *std::string*.

g1 returns *std::string&*, which is a reference to the local variable *str*.

0.70 generalized lambda capture

*** Question 70   generalized lambda capture

What is the output of the program below ?

Program 9: Generalized lambda captures

```
1 #include <iostream>
2
3 int main()
4 {
5     int x = 4;
6
7     auto y = [&r = x, x = x+1]()
```

```
8            {
9                    r += 2;
10                   std::cout << "r is : " << r << std::endl;
11                   return x+2;
12           }();
13
14    std::cout << "y is : " << y << std::endl;
15 }
```

Solution of Question 70

It prints:

```
r is : 6
y is : 7
```

In C++14, lambda capture has been generalized to define arbitrary new local variables in the lambda object because each capture creates a new type-deduced local variable inside the lambda. This enables an init-capture like

```
1 x = std::move(x);
```

the second x must bind to a declaration in the surrounding context.

0.71   generic lambda and product vector

*** Question 71   generic lambda and product vector

Write a generic code to multiply all the elements of a given vector. Generalize it to apply any operation on a vector of any type.

Solution of Question 71

Before C++11, we could write the code for multiplying the contents of a vector of integers as :

Program 10: function object and product vector

```
1 #include <vector>
2 #include <algorithm>
3 #include <iostream>
4
5 int main()
6 {
7     std::vector<int> v{1, 2, 3, 4, 5};
8
9     auto prod =
10        std::accumulate(v.begin(), v.end(),
11                        1,
12                        std::multiplies<int>());
13    std::cout << "product : " << prod << std::endl;
14 }
```

In C++11, we can write the same using lambda as follows:

Program 11: lambda and product vector

```
1 #include <vector>
2 #include <algorithm>
3 #include <iostream>
4
5 int main()
6 {
7     std::vector<int> v{1, 2, 3, 4, 5};
8
9     auto prod =
10        std::accumulate(v.begin(), v.end(),
11                        1,
12                        [](int x, int y) { return x * y; }
13                        );
14    std::cout << "product : " << prod << std::endl;
15 }
```

To generalize with any type, let us write a polymorphic function object :

Program 12: polymorphic function object and product vector

```
1 #include <vector>
2 #include <algorithm>
3 #include <iostream>
4
5 constexpr struct
6 {
7     template< class X, class Y >
8     auto operator () ( X x, Y y )
9         -> decltype(x*y)
10    {
11        return x * y;
12    }
13 } multOp{};
14
15 int main ()
16 {
17     std::vector<int> v{1, 2, 3, 4, 5};
18
19     auto prod =
20         std::accumulate(v.begin(), v.end(),
21                         1,
22                         multOp
23                        );
24     std::cout << "product : " << prod << std::endl;
25 }
```

With C++14 generic lambda, we can write a terse code:

Program 13: generic lambda and product vector

```
1 #include <vector>
2 #include <algorithm>
3 #include <iostream>
4
5 int main ()
6 {
7     std::vector<int> v{1, 2, 3, 4, 5};
8
9     auto prod =
10        std::accumulate(v.begin(), v.end(),
11                        1,
12                        [](auto x, auto y) { return x * y; }
13                       );
14     std::cout << "product : " << prod << std::endl;
15 }
```

Or

Program 14: generic lambda and product vector

```
1 #include <vector>
2 #include <algorithm>
3 #include <iostream>
4
5 auto mult = [](auto x, auto y) { return x * y; };
6
7 int main ()
8 {
9     std::vector<int> v{1, 2, 3, 4, 5};
10
11    auto prod =
12        std::accumulate(v.begin(), v.end(),
13                        1,
14                        mult
15                       );
16    std::cout << "product : " << prod << std::endl;
17 }
```

In C++14, *auto* type-specifier has been allowed to indicate a generic lambda parameter.
Note that this generic lambda-expression containing statement:

```
1 auto mult = [](auto x, auto y) { return x * y; };
```

might result in the creation of a closure type, and object that behaves similar to the *struct* below:

```
1 struct /* anonymous */
2 {
3     template <typename T, typename U>
4     auto operator()(T x, U y) const
5     { return x * y; }
6 } mult;
```

If the initial type-specifier within the decl-specifier-seq of a lambda's parameter declaration is *auto*, the expression creates a *generic lambda closure.*

A generic closure type is just like a familiar C++11 closure type except that its function call operator is a member function template.

In the operator's parameters, each use of *auto* is replaced by a unique template type parameter, which is added to the operator's template-parameter-list as was demonstrated.

0.72 generic lambda

*** Question 72   generic lambda

Write a generic code that accepts an argument of any type and returns the value of its parameter.

Solution of Question 72

Identity is a lambda that accepts an argument of any type and returns the value of its parameter. C++14 generic lambda creates an instance of a class having a function call operator template.

Program 15: usage of generic lambda

```
1 #include <iostream>
2
3 int main()
4 {
5 // 'Identity' is a lambda that accepts an argument of any type and
6 // returns the value of its parameter.
7     auto Identity = [](auto a) { return a; };
8
9     int three_int = Identity(3);
10
11     char const* three_str = Identity("three");
12
13     std::cout << "three as integer : " << three_int << std::endl;
14     std::cout << "three as const char* : " << three_str << std::endl;
15 }
```

It prints:

```
three as integer : 3
three as const char* : three
```

Its conversion to function pointer for capture-less lambdas looks like:

```
1 int (*fpi)(int) = Identity;
2 char (*fpc)(char) = Identity;
```

0.73 generic lambda definition

** Question 73   generic lambda definition

What is *generic lambda* ?

Solution of Question 73

If the *auto* type-specifier appears as one of the decl-specifiers in the decl-specifier-seq of a parameter-declaration of a lambda-expression, the lambda is a *generic lambda*.

For example, the following is a generic lambda:

```
1 auto glambda = [](int i, auto a) { return i; };
2 int& (*fpi)(int*) = [](auto* a) -> auto& { return *a; };
```

This generates a lambda type with a templated *operator()* so that the same lambda object can be invoked with any suitable type and a type-safe function with the right parameter type will be automatically generated.

```
1 std::for_each( std::begin(v), std::end(v), [](const auto& x) { std::cout <<
    x; } );
2 std::sort( std::begin(v), std::end(v), [](const auto& a, const auto& b) {
    return *a<*b; } );
3 auto size = [](const auto& c) { return c.size(); };
```

```
1 auto glambda = [](auto a, auto&& b) { return a < b; };
2 bool b = glambda(3, 3.14);          // OK
3
4 auto vglambda = [](auto printer)
5 {
6     return [=](auto&& ... ts) // OK: ts is a   function parameter pack
7     {
8         printer(std::forward<decltype(ts)>(ts)...);
9
10        return [=]()
11        {
12            printer(ts ...);
13        };
14    };
15 };
16
17 auto p = vglambda( [](auto v1, auto v2, auto v3)  { std::cout << v1 << v2
    << v3; } );
18
19 auto q = p(1, 'a', 3.14);    // OK: outputs 1a3.14
20 q();                          // OK: outputs 1a3.14
```

0.74   conversion function of generic lambda

*** Question 74   conversion function of generic lambda

What can a possible representation of the *generic lambda* given below:

```
1 auto glambda = [](auto a) { return a; };
2 int (*fp)(int) = glambda;
```

Solution of Question 74

The behavior of the conversion function of the *glambda* above is like that of the following conversion function:

Program 16: conversion function of glambda

```
1 struct Closure
2 {
3     template<class T> auto operator()(T t) const { ... }
4     template<class T> static auto lambda_call_operator_invoker(T a)
5     {
6         // forwards execution to operator()(a) and therefore has
7         // the same return type deduced
8         ...
9     }
10
11    template<class T> using fptr_t =
12        decltype(lambda_call_operator_invoker(declval<T>())) (*)(T);
13
14    template<class T> operator fptr_t<T>() const
15    {
16        return &lambda_call_operator_invoker;
17    }
18 };
```

If the generic lambda has no trailing-return-type or the trailing-return-type contains a place-holder type, return type deduction of the corresponding function call operator template specialization has to be done. The corresponding specialization is that instantiation of the function call operator template with the same template arguments as those deduced for the conversion function template.

0.75 generic lambda quiz

** Question 75   generic lambda quiz

What is the output of the following code ?

Program 17: generic lambda revisited

```
1 #include <iostream>
2
3 void f1(int (*)(int))
4 {
5     std::cout << "f1" << std::endl;
6 }
7
8 void f2(char (*)(int))
9 {
10     std::cout << "f2" << std::endl;
11 }
12
13 void g(int (*)(int))
14 {
15     std::cout << "g(int (*)(int))" << std::endl;
16 }
17
18 void g(char (*)(char))
19 {
20     std::cout << "g(char (*)(char))" << std::endl;
21 }
22
23
24 void h(int (*)(int))
25 {
26     std::cout << "h(int (*)(int))" << std::endl;
27 }
28
29 void h(char (*)(int))
30 {
31     std::cout << "h(char (*)(int))" << std::endl;
32 }
33
34
35 // generic lambda
36 auto glambda = [](auto a) { return a; };
37
38
39 int main()
40 {
41     f1(glambda);
42     f2(glambda);
43     g(glambda);
44     h(glambda);
45 }
```

Solution of Question 75

The compiler clang++ 3.5 yields the following error:

```
generic_lambda1.cpp:42:3:
error: no matching function for call to 'f2'
  f2(glambda);
  ^~
generic_lambda1.cpp:8:6:
```

```
note: candidate function not viable: no known
      conversion from
      '(lambda at generic_lambda1.cpp:36:16)'
      to 'char (*)(int)'
      for 1st argument
void f2(char (*)(int))
     ^

generic_lambda1.cpp:43:3:
error: call to 'g' is ambiguous
  g(glambda);
  ^

generic_lambda1.cpp:13:6:
note: candidate function
void g(int (*)(int))
     ^

generic_lambda1.cpp:18:6:
note: candidate function
void g(char (*)(char))
     ^

2 errors generated.
```

Commenting the calls to f2(glambda) and g(glambda), it prints:

```
f1
h(int (*)(int))
```

0.76   Preventing Name Hijacking

*** Question 76   Preventing Name Hijacking

Let us try developing a range structure to help navigate from beginning to end of a given sequence:

```cpp
 1 namespace rng_utils
 2 {
 3     template <class Itr>
 4     struct range
 5     {
 6         Itr begin_, end_;
 7     };
 8
 9     template <class Itr>
10     Itr begin(range<Itr> const & rg)
11     {
12         return rg.begin_;
13     }
14
15     template <class Itr>
16     Itr end(range<Itr> const & rg)
17     {
18         return rg.end_;
19     }
20 }
```

So that it can be used like follows:

```cpp
42     rng_utils::range<int *> r;
43
44     for(int i : r)
45     {
46         std::cout << i << std::endl;
47     }
```

Motivated by this design, a typical usage framework for a given task may look like:

```cpp
24 namespace tasks
25 {
```

```
26      template <class TaskLike>
27      void begin(TaskLike && t)
28      {
29          t.begin();
30      }
31
32      struct Task
33      {
34          void Begin()
35          {}
36      };
37 }
```

Followed by its usage scenario:

```
49      rng_utils::range<tasks::Task *> r1;
50
51      for(tasks::Task t : r1)
52      {
53          t.Begin();
54      }
```

Can you spot what is wrong with this code ?

Solution of Question 76

It does not compile.
clang 3.5 error is:

```
adl_overload.cpp:51:23:
error: cannot use type 'void' as an iterator
    for(tasks::Task t : r1)
                        ^
adl_overload.cpp:27:10:
note: selected 'begin' template [with TaskLike =
      rng_utils::range<tasks::Task *> &] with iterator type 'void'
    void begin(TaskLike && t)
         ^
adl_overload.cpp:29:11: error: no member named 'begin' in
      'rng_utils::range<tasks::Task *>'
        t.begin();
        ~ ^
adl_overload.cpp:51:23:
note: in instantiation of function template
 specialization 'tasks::begin<rng_utils::range<tasks::Task *> &>'
requested here
    for(tasks::Task t : r1)
                        ^

2 errors generated.
```

gcc 4.9 error :

```
adl_overload.cpp: In function 'int main()':
adl_overload.cpp:51:25:
error: inconsistent begin/end types in
range-based 'for' statement: 'void' and 'tasks::Task*'
    for(tasks::Task t : r1)
                        ^
adl_overload.cpp:51:25:
error: 'void __for_begin' has incomplete type
adl_overload.cpp:51:25:
error: 'void __for_end' has incomplete type
adl_overload.cpp: In instantiation of
'void tasks::begin(TaskLike&&)
 [with TaskLike = rng_utils::range<tasks::Task*>&]':
adl_overload.cpp:51:25:   required from here
adl_overload.cpp:29:9:
```

```
error: 'struct rng_utils::range<tasks::Task*>'
has no member named 'begin'
          t.begin();
```

Both of these errors point out to the issue of wrong overload being selected due to unintentional ADL.

We have to find a way to prevent name hijacking.

Use a non-inline ADL-blocking namespace

```
24 namespace tasks
25 {
26     template <class TaskLike>
27     void begin(TaskLike && t)
28     {
29         t.begin();
30     }
31
32     namespace block_adl
33     {
34         struct Task
35         {
36             void Begin()
37             {}
38         };
39     }
40     using block_adl::Task;
41 }
```

Note that we have put the type definition for *Task* in an ADL blocking namespace.

So the lesson is : *Put type definitions in an ADL-blocking (non-inline!) namespaces and export then with a using declaration.*

Use global function objects instead of free functions

Fortunately, there is another way to solve this problem. We can use global function objects instead of free functions:

```
24 namespace tasks
25 {
26     constexpr struct begin_fn
27     {
28         template <class TaskLike>
29         void operator()(TaskLike && t) const
30         {
31             t.Begin();
32         }
33     } begin {};
34
35     struct Task
36     {
37         void Begin()
38         {}
39     };
40 }
```

Note that the *begin* object cannot ever be found by ADL.

So the function objects are good in this case because:

- They are never found by ADL.
- If phase 1 lookup finds an object instead of a function, ADL is disabled.
- They are first class objects: Easy to bind and Easy to pass to higher-order functions like *std::accumulate*.

So the lesson is : *Prefer global constexpr function objects over named free functions.*

In C++14, we can use *Variable Templates*:

```
24 namespace tasks
25 {
26     template <typename T>
27     struct begin_fn
28     {
29         template <class TaskLike>
30         void operator()(TaskLike && t) const
31         {
32             t.Begin();
33         }
34     };
35
36     template <typename T>
37     constexpr begin_fn<T> begin{};
38
39     struct Task
40     {
41         void Begin()
42         {}
43     };
44 }
```

0.77   Find First Null Pointer in a Container

** Question 77   Find First Null Pointer in a Container

Write a function *findNull*, which would return an iterator to the first null pointer or the end iterator if none is found for a given container of pointers.

Solution of Question 77

In C++98, the typical code would look like:

```
1 #include <iostream>
2 #include <vector>
3
4 template<typename Container>
5 typename Container::const_iterator findNull(const Container &c)
6 {
7     typename Container::const_iterator iter;
8     for (iter = c.begin(); iter != c.end(); ++iter)
9         if (*iter == 0)
10             break;
11
12     return iter;
13 }
14
15 int main()
16 {
17     int a = 10, b = 20, c = 30, d = 40;
18
19     std::vector<int *> v;
20
21     v.push_back(&a);
22     v.push_back(&b);
23     v.push_back(&c);
24     v.push_back(0);
25     v.push_back(&d);
26
27     std::vector<int *>::const_iterator cit = findNull(v);
28
29     if (cit == v.end())
30         std::cout << "no null pointers in v" << std::endl;
31     else
32     {
33         std::vector<int *>::difference_type pos = cit - v.begin();
34         std::cout << "null pointer found at pos. " << pos << std::endl;
35     }
36 }
```

It prints:

```
null pointer found at pos. 3
```

It is very verbose. In C++11, we can reduce this a bit. Our client code would look like :

```cpp
int main()
{
    int a = 10, b = 20, c = 30, d  = 40;

    std::vector<int *> v { &a, &b, &c, 0, &d };

    auto cit = findNull(v);

    if (cit == v.end())
        std::cout << "no null pointers in v" << std::endl;
    else
    {
        auto pos = cit - v.begin();
        std::cout << "null pointer found at pos. " << pos << std::endl;
    }
}
```

Let us recall a well cited problem related to marking the return type because sometimes a return type simply cannot be expressed in the usual manner:

```cpp
// Function template to return product of two values of unknown types:
template<typename T, typename U>
??? product(const T &t, const U &u)
{
    return t * u;
}
```

In this case, a combination of *auto*, *decltype* and *trailing return type* provide the only solution for C++11:

```cpp
// Function template to return product of two values of unknown types:
template<typename T, typename U>
auto product(const T &t, const U &u)
    -> decltype(t * u)
{
    return t * u;
}
```

So we can rewrite our function *findNull* in C++11 as follows:

```cpp
template<typename Cont>
auto findNull(const Cont &c)
    -> decltype(c.begin())
{
    auto it = c.begin();
    for (; it != c.end(); ++it)
        if (*it == 0)
            break;
    return it;
}
```

Is this all we can do in C++11 ?

Fortunately , there is *Non-Member begin/ end*, which are new forms of *begin()* and *end()*, which even work for native arrays, hence are more generalized.

```cpp
#include <iostream>
#include <cstring>
#include <vector>
#include <algorithm>

bool strLenGT4(const char *s) { return std::strlen(s) > 4; }

int main()
{
    // Applied to STL container:
    std::vector<int> v {-5, -16, 3, 10, 15, 50, 200};
```

```
12
13     auto first3 = std::find(std::begin(v), std::end(v), 3);
14
15     if (first3 != std::end(v))
16         std::cout << "First 3 in v = " << *first3 << std::endl;
17
18     // Applied to native array:
19     const char *names[] {"Chan", "Chandra", "Shekhar"};
20
21     auto firstGT4 = std::find_if( std::begin(names), std::end(names),
           strLenGT4);
22
23     if (firstGT4 != std::end(names))
24         std::cout << "First long name: " << *firstGT4 << std::endl;
25 }
```

In C++14, there are Non-Member begin/ end variations:

- Return const_iterators: *cbegin/cend*
- Return reverse_iterators: *rbegin/rend*
- Return const_reverse_iterators: *crbegin/crend*

Allowing us to write code like:

```
1 template <typename Container>
2 void process_container(Container &c) // Note: no const
3 {
4     typename C::const_iterator ci = std::begin(c); // C++11
5     auto ci2 = std::cbegin(c); // C++14
6     . . .
7 }
```

Oh, we missed the problem associated with representation of null pointers. In old C++, the concept of *null pointers* can be a source of confusion and ambiguity. How is *NULL* defined? Does *0* refer to an *int* or a *pointer*?

```
1 void f(long) { cout << "f(long)\n"; }
2 void f(char *) { cout << "f(char *)\n";}
3
4 int main()
5 {
6     f(0L); // calls f(long)
7     f(0); // ERROR: ambiguous!
8     f(static_cast<char *>(0)); // ok
9 }
```

in C++14, we can use *nullptr* instead of 0 to help disambiguate:

```
1 void f(long) { cout << "f(long)\n"; }
2 void f(char *) { cout << "f(char *)\n";}
3 int main()
4 {
5     f(0L); // as before, calls f(long)
6     f(nullptr); // fine, calls f(char *)
7     f(0); // still ambiguous
8 }
```

So we can rewrite our function *findNull* in C++11 as:

```
1 template<typename Cont>
2 auto findNull(const Cont &c)
3     -> decltype(begin(c))
4 {
5     auto it = begin(c);
6     for (; it != end(c); ++it)
7         if (*it == nullptr)
8             break;
9     return it;
10 }
```

In C++14, there is support for *Generalized Function Return Type Deduction* allowing return type to be deduced from the return expression(s) used:

```
1 template<typename Cont>
2 auto findNull(const Cont &c) // we don't need decltype!
3 {
4     auto it = begin(c);
5     for (; it != end(c); ++it)
6         if (*it == nullptr)
7             break;
8     return it;    // return type deduced HERE
9 }
```

There are actually two approaches to function return type deduction in C++14:

1. Functions declared to return *auto* (or "decorated" *auto*) : employs template type deduction rules, discards references, const, volatile from return expression's type (may add it back when *auto* is decorated).

2. Function declared to return *decltype(auto)* : no decoration permitted, employs *decltype* type deduction, expression's actual type is the return type.

0.78   Generic Operator Functors

*** Question 78   Generic Operator Functors

Sort a vector of integers in descending order. Extend the logic to the vectors of unsigned 32-bit integers, 64-bit integers and const char * respectively.

Solution of Question 78

Sounds like a trivial operation. We can use the function object *std::greater* as follows:

```
1 #include <functional>
2 #include <vector>
3 #include <algorithm>
4 #include <cassert>
5
6 int main()
7 {
8     std::vector<int> v {5, 1, 6, 3, 4, 2};
9     std::sort(v.begin(), v.end(), std::greater<int>());
10     assert( v == std::vector<int> ({6, 5, 4, 3, 2, 1}));
11 }
```

Quick inside into the implementation of *std::greater* :

```
1 template <class T>
2 struct greater : binary_function<T, T, bool>
3 {
4     bool operator()(const T & x, const T& y) const
5         {return x > y;}
6 };
```

Typical usage :

```
1     typedef std::greater<int> F;
2     const F f = F();
3
4     static_assert((std::is_base_of<std::binary_function<int, int, bool>, F
        >::value), "");
5
6     assert(!f(36, 36));
7     assert(f(36, 6));
8     assert(!f(6, 36));
```

We could take leverage of lambda functions as well:

```
1 #include <vector>
2 #include <algorithm>
3 #include <cassert>
4
5 int main()
6 {
```

```
7      std :: vector<int> v {5, 1, 6, 3, 4, 2};
8      std :: sort (v.begin(), v.end(),
9          [](const int & l, const int & r)
10         { return l > r; });
11     assert( v == std :: vector<int> ({6, 5, 4, 3, 2, 1}));
12 }
```

It is not difficult to see that lambda approach is not just a bit mouthful, but it is difficult to use it with associative containers like *std::map*, where we can easily write the same using the function object *std::greater* :

```
std :: map<KeyType, ValueType, std :: greater<KeyType>>
```

Astute reader must have noticed that the stated usage requires the user to specify its argument type explicitly though the compiler already has this information at the point of functor invocation. This is a bit verbose which we would to get rid of.

Proceeding further, extending our hand to vector of *uint_32* :

```
std :: vector<uint32_t> vu_32;
// fill in the vector ... then sort as usual
std :: sort (vu_32.begin(), vu_32.end(), std :: greater<uint32_t>());
```

Suppose the vector is changed to

```
std :: vector<uint64_t> vu_64;
```

But suppose the user forgot to incorporate this in *std::greater*, i.e., *std::greater<uint32_t>* (), so that the *std::vector<uint64_t>* gets sorted with *std::greater<uint32_t>* (), then the elements will be truncated before being compared. The compiler may emit a truncation warning, but it would be better to make this scenario completely impossible.

Now, let us try to work with *std::vector<const char *>*.

```
1 #include <functional>
2 #include <vector>
3 #include <algorithm>
4 #include <cassert>
5
6 int main()
7 {
8      std :: vector<const char *> v {"a", "abc", "ab"};
9      std :: sort (v.begin(), v.end(), std :: greater<const char *>());
10     assert( v == std :: vector<const char *> ({"abc", "ab", "a"}));
11 }
```

But it does not work because *std::greater<const char *>* compares pointers. So we need to change to *std::vector<std::string>*:

```
1 #include <functional>
2 #include <vector>
3 #include <algorithm>
4 #include <cassert>
5
6 int main()
7 {
8      std :: vector<const char *> v {"a", "abc", "ab"};
9      std :: sort (v.begin(), v.end(), std :: greater<std :: string>());
10     assert( v == std :: vector<const char *> ({"abc", "ab", "a"}));
11 }
```

But this is inefficient because every invocation of *std::greater<std::string>*'s function call operator will construct a temporary *std::string* from elem. This inefficiency is a direct result of the homogeneous signature like *T (const T&, const T&)* not being *transparent*.

The problems are getting piled up so far. We badly need a templated function call operator, capable of accepting arbitrary argument types along with being perfectly forwarding and perfectly returning.

Fortunately C++14 provides *std::greater<>* which addresses all of these issues nicely by providing the needed functionality.

```
std :: sort (v.begin(), v.end(), std :: greater<>());
```

Typical usage :

```
1    typedef std::greater<> F2;
2    const F2 f2 = F2();
3
4    assert(!f2(36, 36));
5    assert(f2(36, 6));
6    assert(!f2(6, 36));
7    assert( f2(36, 6.0));
8    assert( f2(36.0, 6));
9    assert(!f2(6, 36.0));
10   assert(!f2(6.0, 36));
11
12   constexpr bool foo = std::greater<int>() (36, 36);
13   static_assert ( !foo, "" );
14
15   constexpr bool bar = std::greater<> () (36.0, 36);
16   static_assert ( !bar, "" );
```

Quick inside into C++14 implementation of *std::greater* :

```
1  template <class T = void>
2  struct greater : binary_function<T, T, bool>
3  {
4      bool operator()(const T & x, const T& y) const
5      {
6          return x > y;
7      }
8  };
9
10 template<>
11 struct greater<void>
12 {
13     template <typename T, typename U>
14     auto operator()(T && t, U && u) const
15         noexcept(noexcept(std::forward<T>(t) > std::forward<U>(u)))
16             -> decltype(std::forward<T>(t) > std::forward<U>(u))
17     {
18         return std::forward<T>(t) > std::forward<U>(u);
19     }
20 };
```

All of the perfectly forwarding function call operators are also perfectly returning, even those for the comparators.

C++14 provides extends this to other functors as well like plus, minus, equal_to etc allowing us the code like:

```
1  #include <algorithm>
2  #include <iostream>
3  #include <iterator>
4  #include <ostream>
5  #include <set>
6  #include <string>
7  #include <vector>
8
9  int main()
10 {
11     std::vector<const char *> v {"3", "2", "1"};
12
13     std::set<std::string, std::greater<>> s {"a", "aaa", "aa"};
14
15     std::vector<std::string> dest;
16
17     std::transform(v.begin(), v.end(), s.begin(),
18         std::back_inserter(dest), std::plus<>());
19
20     for (const auto& elem : dest)
21     {
22         std::cout << elem << std::endl;
23     }
24 }
```

It prints:

```
3aaa
2aa
1a
```

C++14 also provides a new addition *std::bit_xor* :

```
1 template <class T = void> struct bit_xor;
2
3 template <> struct bit_xor<void>
4 {
5     template <class T, class U> auto operator()(T&& t, U&& u) const
6         -> decltype(std::forward<T>(t) ^ std::forward<U>(u))
7     {
8         return std::forward<T>(t) ^ std::forward<U>(u);
9     }
10 };
```

Astute reader may notice that the technique of using default template arguments and explicit specializations for *void* was chosen for its non-intrusiveness. Moreover *std::greater< void >* isn't valid in C++11 because it would attempt to form a reference to void, which is forbidden.

0.79 Exchange Utility

** Question 79   Exchange Utility

Develop an utility which assigns a new value to the supplied object and returns the old value as well as:

- avoids copying the old value when that type defines a move constructor
- accepts any type as the new value, taking advantage of any converting assignment operator and
- avoids copying the new value if it's a temporary or moved.

Solution of Question 79

C++14 provides an utility *std::exchange* which fulfills these criteria.
Typical implementation looks like:

```
1 template<class T1, class T2 = T1>
2 inline T1 exchange(T1 & obj, T2 && new_value)
3 {
4     T1 old_value = std::move(obj);
5
6     obj = std::forward<T2>(new_value);
7
8     return old_value;
9 }
```

Typical usage:

```
1 #include <utility>
2 #include <cassert>
3 #include <string>
4
5 int main()
6 {
7     {
8         int v = 12;
9         assert ( std::exchange ( v, 23 ) == 12 );
10        assert ( v == 23 );
11        assert ( std::exchange ( v, 67.2 ) == 23 );
12        assert ( v == 67 );
13
14        assert ((std::exchange<int, float> ( v, {} )) == 67 );
15        assert ( v == 0 );
16    }
17
18    {
19        bool b = false;
```

```
20          assert ( !std::exchange ( b, true ));
21          assert ( b );
22      }
23
24      {
25          const std::string s1 ( "Hi Mom!" );
26          const std::string s2 ( "Yo Dad!" );
27
28          std::string s3 = s1;
29
30          assert ( std::exchange ( s3, s2 ) == s1 );
31          assert ( s3 == s2 );
32
33          assert ( std::exchange ( s3, "Hi Mom!" ) == s2 );
34          assert ( s3 == s1 );
35
36          s3 = s2;
37
38          assert ( std::exchange ( s3, {} ) == s2 );
39          assert ( s3.size () == 0 );
40          s3 = s2;
41
42          assert ( std::exchange ( s3, "" ) == s2 );
43          assert ( s3.size () == 0 );
44      }
45
46      {
47          const unsigned val = 4;
48          int i = 1;
49          auto prev = std::exchange(i, val);
50
51          static_assert( std::is_same<decltype(prev), int >::value, "return
                type" );
52          assert( i == 4 );
53          assert( prev == 1 );
54
55          prev = std::exchange(i, 3);
56
57          assert( i == 3 );
58          assert( prev == 4 );
59      }
60 }
```

It works with user defined types as well:

```
1 #include <utility>
2 #include <cassert>
3
4 struct DefaultConstructible
5 {
6      DefaultConstructible(int i = 0) : value(i) { }
7      int value;
8 };
9
10 struct From { };
11
12 struct To
13 {
14      int value = 0;
15
16      To() = default;
17      To(const To&) = default;
18      To(const From&) = delete;
19
20      To& operator=(const From&)
21      {
22          value = 1; return *this;
23      }
24
25      To& operator=(From&&)
26      {
27          value = 2; return *this;
28      }
29 };
```

```
30
31
32 int  main ()
33 {
34      DefaultConstructible  x = 1;
35
36      auto  old = std::exchange(x, {});
37
38      assert ( x.value == 0 );
39      assert ( old.value == 1 );
40
41      To  t;
42      From  f;
43
44      auto  prev = std::exchange(t, f);
45
46      assert ( t.value == 1 );
47      assert ( prev.value == 0 );
48
49      prev = std::exchange(t, From{});
50
51      assert ( t.value == 2 );
52      assert ( prev.value == 1 );
53 }
```

    std::exchange is capable to deduce type of overloaded function:

```
1 #include <utility>
2 #include <cassert>
3
4 int  f(int)  { return 0; }
5
6 double  f(double)  { return 0; }
7
8 int  (*fp)(int);
9
10 int  main ()
11 {
12    std::exchange(fp, &f);
13    assert ( fp != nullptr );
14 }
```

    It helps rewrite the implementation of *reset* member function of
std::unique_ptr.
    Typical implementation:

```
1 template<typename T, typename D>
2 void  unique_ptr<T, D>::reset(pointer p = pointer())
3 {
4    pointer old = ptr_;
5    ptr_ = p;
6    if (old)
7      deleter_(old);
8 }
```

    Recommended implementation:

```
1 template<typename T, typename D>
2 void  unique_ptr<T, D>::reset(pointer p = pointer())
3 {
4    if (pointer old = std::exchange(ptr_, p))
5      deleter_(old);
6 }
```

0.80 Addressing Tuple By Type

*** Question 80   Addressing Tuple By Type

Suppose there is a function *get_order* that returns a

std::tuple<date, **std::map**<item, **int**>>

representing an order placed by a company. Find a point on a graph, where the x coordinate is the day number of the *date* and the y coordinate is the total number of items in the order.

Assume that there is a function which computes the day number for a given date:

```
int days_from_epoch(date d);
```

And *item* is represented by :

```
struct item
{
    item(int i) : itemid(i) {}
    int itemid;
};
```

Solution of Question 80

In order to add up all the order counts, let us have a convenient alias template for our map:

```
template<class Key, class Value>
    using map_t =
        std::map<Key, Value, std::function<bool(const Key&, const Key&)>>;
```

Now, it becomes easy to supply desired comparators on the fly using lambda :

```
map_t<item, int> orderitemidtems {
        [](const item & a, const item & b)
        { return a.itemid < b.itemid; }
    };
orderitemidtems = {{1, 10}, {2, 20}, {3, 30}};
```

Adding up all the order counts :

```
int items_in_order(const map_t<item, int> & orderitemidtems)
{
    return std::accumulate(orderitemidtems.begin(), orderitemidtems.end(),
        0,
        [](int acc, std::pair<item, int> const & p) { return acc + p.second
            ; });
}
```

Note that the following snippet will print 60:

```
std::cout << items_in_order(orderitemidtems);
```

Our final code would look like:

```
auto point = std::make_tuple(days_from_epoch, items_in_order)(get_order(/*
    ... */));
```

This is possible because C++14 allows tuples to be addressed by type as well as by numerical index like:

```
tuple<string, string, int> t("foo", "bar", 7);
int i = get<int>(t); // i == 7
int j = get<2>(t); // Equivalent to the above: j == 7
string s = get<string>(t); // Compile−time error. Ambiguous

const tuple<int, const int, double, double> t(1, 2, 3.4, 5.6);
const int &i1 = get<int>(t);       // OK. Not ambiguous. i1 == 1
const int &i2 = get<const int>(t); // OK. Not ambiguous. i2 == 2
const double &d = get<double>(t);  // ERROR. ill−formed
```

It also allows writing code like :

```
auto funcs = make_tuple(sqrt, strlen, atof);
auto vals = make_tuple(9, "foo", "7.3");
auto result = funcs(vals); // result is tuple<double, size_t, double>(3, 3,
    7.3)
```

as well as:

```
auto funcs =
    make_tuple(bind(std::multiplies<int, int>, _1, _1),
               function(&string::size),
               [](char const *cp)->double
               {
                   istringstream is(cp);
                   double d;
                   is >> d;
                   return d;
               });
auto vals = make_tuple(9, "foo", "7.3");
auto result = funcs(vals); // result is tuple<int, size_t, double>(81, 3,
    7.3)
```

0.81   Quoted manipulators

** Question 81   Quoted manipulators

What is the output of the program below ? Modify the program if needed to rectify issues if any.

```
1 #include <sstream>
2 #include <iostream>
3
4 int main()
5 {
6     std::stringstream ss;
7     std::string original = "Chandra Shekhar Kumar";
8
9     std::string round_trip;
10
11    ss << original;
12    ss >> round_trip;
13
14    std::cout << original << std::endl;
15    std::cout << round_trip << std::endl;
16 }
```

Solution of Question 81

It prints:

```
Chandra Shekhar Kumar
Chandra
```

The output is not what we expected and it looks like that the standard library stream I/O has a problem with embedded spaces in strings.

Fortunately, C++14 introduced *quoted* stream I/O manipulator which places delimiters, defaulted to double-quote ("), around strings on output, and strips off the delimiters on input. This ensures strings with embedded white space round-trip as desired.

So the modified program meeting our expectation is as follows:

```
1 #include <sstream>
2 #include <iomanip>
3 #include <iostream>
4
5 int main()
6 {
7     std::stringstream ss;
8     std::string original = "Chandra Shekhar Kumar";
9
10    std::string round_trip;
11
12    ss << quoted(original);
13    ss >> quoted(round_trip);
14
15    std::cout << original << std::endl;
16    std::cout << round_trip << std::endl;
17 }
```

Quoted manipulators provide string insertion and extraction of quoted strings and ensures that the content of a string with embedded spaces remains unchanged if inserted and then extracted via stream I/O.

```
template<typename CharT>
inline auto quoted(const CharT* s,
                        CharT delim = CharT('"'),
                        CharT escape = CharT('\\'));

template<typename CharT, typename Traits, typename Alloc>
inline auto quoted(const basic_string<CharT, Traits, Alloc>& s,
                        CharT delim = CharT('"'),
                        CharT escape = CharT('\\'));
```

If *out* is an instance of *basic_ostream* with member type *char_type* the same as *CharT*, then the expression

out << quoted(s, delim, escape)

behaves as if it inserts the following characters into *out* using character inserter function templates:

- delim.
- Each character in *s*. If the character to be output is equal to *escape* or *delim*, as determined by *operator==*, first output *escape*.
- *delim*.

Type of the following expression

out << quoted(s, delim, escape)

is

std::basic_ostream<CharT, Traits>&

and value *out*.

```
template<typename CharT, typename Traits, typename Alloc>
inline auto quoted(basic_string<CharT, Traits, Alloc>& s,
                        CharT delim = CharT('"'),
                        CharT escape = CharT('\\'));
```

If *in* is an instance of *basic_istream* with member type *char_type* the same as *CharT*, then the expression

in >> quoted(s, delim, escape)

behaves as if it extracts the following characters from *in* using

basic_istream::**operator>>**

- If the first character extracted is equal to *delim*, as determined by *operator==*, then:
  - Turn off the *skipws* flag.
  - s.clear()
  - Until an unescaped *delim* character is reached or *!in*, extract characters from *in* and append them to *s*, except that if an *escape* is reached, ignore it and append the next character to *s*.
  - Discard the final *delim* character.
  - Restore the *skipws* flag to its original value.
- Otherwise, *in* >> *s*.

If *out* is an instance of *basic_ostream* with member type *char_type* the same as *CharT*, then the expression

out << quoted(s, delim, escape)

behaves as specified for the

const basic_string<charT, traits, Allocator>&

overload of the quoted function.

Implementation of Quoted Manipulators

Typical implementation may look like:

Program 18: Structure for delimited strings

```
template<typename String, typename CharT>
struct Quotedstring
{
    static_assert(std::is_reference<String>::value
                    || std::is_pointer<String>::value,
                        "String type must be pointer or reference");

    Quotedstring(String str, CharT del, CharT esc)
        : M_string(str), M_delim{del}, M_escape{esc}
    { }

    Quotedstring& operator=(Quotedstring&) = delete;

    String M_string;
    CharT M_delim;
    CharT M_escape;
};
```

Note that the left and right delimiters can be different.

Program 19: Inserter for delimited strings

```
template<typename CharT, typename Traits>
auto& operator<<(std::basic_ostream<CharT, Traits>& os,
    const Quotedstring<const CharT*, CharT>& str)
{
    os << str._M_delim;
    for (const CharT* c = str.M_string; *c; ++c)
    {
        if (*c == str.M_delim || *c == str.M_escape)
            os << str.M_escape;

        os << *c;
    }
    os << str.M_delim;

    return os;
}

template<typename CharT, typename Traits, typename String>
auto& operator<<(std::basic_ostream<CharT, Traits>& os,
    const Quotedstring<const CharT*, CharT>& str)
{
    os << str._M_delim;
    for (auto & c = str.M_string)
    {
        if (c == str.M_delim || c == str.M_escape)
            os << str.M_escape;

        os << c;
    }
    os << str.M_delim;

    return os;
}
```

Program 20: Extractor for delimited strings

```
template<typename CharT, typename Traits, typename Alloc>
auto& operator>>(std::basic_istream<CharT, Traits>& is,
    const Quotedstring<basic_string<CharT, Traits, Alloc>&, CharT>& str)
{
    CharT c;
    is >> c;

    if (!is.good())
```

```
9         return is;
10
11      if (c != str.M_delim)
12      {
13          is.unget();
14          is >> str.M_string;
15          return is;
16      }
17
18      str.M_string.clear();
19
20      std::ios_base::fmtflags flags
21          = is.flags(is.flags() & ~std::ios_base::skipws);
22
23      do
24      {
25          is >> c;
26          if (!is.good())
27              break;
28          if (c == str.M_escape)
29          {
30              is >> c;
31              if (!is.good())
32                  break;
33          }
34          else if (c == str.M_delim)
35              break;
36          str.M_string += c;
37      }
38      while (true);
39
40      is.setf(__flags);
41
42      return is;
43 }
```

```
1 template<typename CharT>
2 inline auto
3 quoted(const CharT* string,
4   CharT delim = CharT('"'), CharT escape = CharT('\\'))
5 {
6   return Quotedstring<const CharT*, CharT>(string, delim, escape);
7 }
8
9 template<typename CharT, typename Traits, typename Alloc>
10 inline auto
11 quoted(const basic_string<CharT, Traits, Alloc>& string,
12   CharT delim = CharT('"'), CharT escape = CharT('\\'))
13 {
14   return Quotedstring<
15     const basic_string<CharT, Traits, Alloc>&, CharT>(string, delim, escape
          );
16 }
17
18 template<typename CharT, typename Traits, typename Alloc>
19 inline auto
20 quoted(basic_string<CharT, Traits, Alloc>& string,
21   CharT delim = CharT('"'), CharT escape = CharT('\\'))
22 {
23   return Quotedstring<
24     basic_string<CharT, Traits, Alloc>&, CharT>(string, delim, escape);
25 }
```

It allows to write code like:

```
1 std::string quote ( const char *p, char delim='"', char escape='\\' )
2 {
3     std::stringstream ss;
4     ss << std::quoted(p, delim, escape);
5     std::string s;
6     ss >> s;    // no quote
```

```
7      return s;
8 }
9
10 assert ( quote ( "Hi", '!' ) == "!Hi!" );
11 assert ( quote ( "Hi!", '!' ) == R"(!Hi\!!)" );
12 assert ( quote ( "" ) == "\"\"" );
13 assert ( quote ( "a" ) == "\"a\"" );
```

0.82 Null Iterator

** Question 82   Null Iterator

Design a class hierarchy that provides iterator access to a member *vector*, along with other features.
The base class does not actually have a vector, but some derived classes do.

Solution of Question 82

Typical Interface may look like:

```
1 struct A
2 {
3      virtual std::vector<int>::const_iterator begin();
4      virtual std::vector<int>::const_iterator end();
5 };
6
7 struct B : A
8 {
9      virtual std::vector<int>::const_iterator begin();
10      virtual std::vector<int>::const_iterator end();
11
12      std::vector<int> v;
13 };
```

It is not difficult to complete the design of derived class *B*:

```
1 struct B : A
2 {
3      explicit B(std::vector<int> & _v) : v(_v) {}
4
5      virtual std::vector<int>::const_iterator begin()
6      {
7          return v.begin();
8      }
9
10      virtual std::vector<int>::const_iterator end()
11      {
12          return v.end();
13      }
14
15      std::vector<int> v;
16 };
```

But how to do something similar with the base class A because there is no vector to point to.
So the real challenge is to create a valid iterator without a container instance.

C++14 provides support for *null iterators* by allowing *value-initialized forward iterators* to be
compared, and ensuring that all value-initialized iterators for a particular container type compare
equal. The result of comparing a value-initialized iterator to an iterator with a non-singular value
is undefined.

So our base class looks like:

```
1 struct A
2 {
3      A() {}
4      virtual std::vector<int>::const_iterator begin()
5      {
6          return {};
7      }
8
9      virtual std::vector<int>::const_iterator end()
```

```
10      {
11          return  {};
12      }
13 };
```

It allows writing code like:

```
1 #include <vector>
2 #include <cassert>
3
4 int main()
5 {
6      typedef std::vector<int> C;
7      C::iterator ii1{}, ii2{};
8      C::iterator ii4 = ii1;
9      C::const_iterator cii{};
10     assert( ii1 == ii2 );
11     assert( ii1 == ii4 );
12
13     assert(!( ii1 != ii2 ));
14
15     assert( (ii1 == cii ));
16     assert( (cii == ii1 ));
17     assert(!( ii1 != cii ));
18     assert(!( cii != ii1 ));
19     assert(!( ii1 <  cii ));
20     assert(!( cii <  ii1 ));
21     assert( (ii1 <= cii ));
22     assert( (cii <= ii1 ));
23     assert(!( ii1 >  cii ));
24     assert(!( cii >  ii1 ));
25     assert( (ii1 >= cii ));
26     assert( (cii >= ii1 ));
27     assert( cii - ii1 == 0);
28     assert( ii1 - cii == 0);
29 }
```

0.83   std::move is rvalue_cast

*** Question 83   std::move is rvalue_cast

Explain how *std::move* works and provide implementation details.

Solution of Question 83

std::move doesn't guarantee move, it just unconditionally casts to an *rvalue*, so it can be treated as a *rvalue_cast*.

A possible implementation may look like:

```
1 template<typename T>
2 constexpr typename std::remove_reference<T>::type&&
3 move(T&& t) noexcept
4 {
5     return
6     static_cast<typename std::remove_reference<T>::type&&>(t);
7 }
```

In C++14, it can be simplified further to:

```
1 template<typename T>
2 decltype(auto)
3 move(T&& t) noexcept
4 {
5     return
6     static_cast<std::remove_reference_t<T>&&>(t);
7 }
```

It is recommended not to declare objects as *const* with *std::move*.
Let us take an example:

```
A a;
std::move(a); // a is lvalue
```

Recall that An *lvalue* is an expression with which we can use & operator. An *rvalue* is an expression that is not an *lvalue*.

Objects that are declared as *rvalue reference*, &&, can be lvalues or rvalues. If it has a name, then it is an lvalue. Otherwise, it is an rvalue.

Reference collapsing : If a typedef-name or a decltype-specifier denotes a type *TR* that is a reference to a type *T*, an attempt to create the type *lvalue reference to cv TR* creates the type *lvalue reference to T*, while an attempt to create the type *rvalue reference to cv TR* creates the type TR.

- *T& &* becomes *T&*
- *T& &&* becomes *T&*
- *T&& &* becomes *T&*
- *T&& &&* becomes *T&&*

```
int i;
typedef int& LRI;
typedef int&& RRI;

LRI& r1 = i; // r1 has the type int&
const LRI& r2 = i; // r2 has the type int&
const LRI&& r3 = i; // r3 has the type int&

RRI& r4 = i; // r4 has the type int&
RRI&& r5 = 5; // r5 has the type int&&

decltype(r2)& r6 = i; // r6 has the type int&
decltype(r2)&& r7 = i; // r7 has the type int&
```

There is a special template argument deduction rule for function templates that take an argument by *rvalue reference* to a template argument:

```
template<typename T>
void f(T&&);
```

Here, the following apply:

- When *f* is called on an lvalue of type *A*, then *T* resolves to *A&* and hence, by the reference collapsing rules above, the argument type effectively becomes *A&*.
- When *f* is called on an rvalue of type *A*, then *T* resolves to *A*, and hence the argument type becomes *A&&*.

By this special template deduction rule, the template argument *T* will resolve to *A&*. After evaluating the *remove_reference* and applying the reference collapsing rules, we get

```
A&& std::move(A& a) noexcept
{
    return static_cast<A&&>(a);
}
```

So, the lvalue a will bind to the lvalue reference that is the argument type, and the function passes it right through, turning it into an unnamed rvalue reference. Simple !

0.84 C++14 Compiler

*** Question 84   C++14 Compiler

How to get a C++14 Compiler ?

Solution of Question 84

There are plenty of compilers available for free. Pick one which suits you.

- *Gnu Compiler Collection : gcc 4.9.0* : Easy steps for installing GCC 4.9.0:

- wget ftp://ftp.gnu.org/gnu/gcc/gcc-4.9.0/ gcc-4.9.0.tar.bz2
- tar -xvjf gcc-4.9.0.tar.bz2
- cd gcc-4.9.0
- ./contrib/download_prerequisites
- cd ..
- mkdir gcc-4.9.0-build
- cd gcc-4.9.0-build
- $PWD/../gcc-4.9.0/configure –enable-languages=c,c++
- make -j$(nproc)
  Here nproc is the number of processors.
- make install
  This will install gcc-4.9.0 in the path /usr/local/bin. *g++* is the C++ compiler.

- *Clang 3.5*: A new open-source C++ compiler for various platforms. Kindly note that you may need to include the latest libstdc++ in your path to help clang build environment search it appropriately. On Linux-like systems, it could be achieved by including the following somewhere(eg, .bashrc):

  ```
  export LD_LIBRARY_PATH=
  /usr/local/lib:$LD_LIBRARY_PATH
  ```

  In 64-bit systems, it may be:

  ```
  export LD_LIBRARY_PATH=
  /usr/local/lib64:$LD_LIBRARY_PATH
  ```

- Online Compilers:

  - gcc.godbolt.org (Clang, GCC, Intel ICC)
  - Rise4Fun (Microsoft VC++)
  - Stacked-Crooked (GCC)
  - Rextester (Clang, GCC)
  - ideone.com (GCC)

clang++ is the C++ compiler.

For C++11 features, the option is *-std=c++11*.

For C++14 features, the option is *-std=c+1y*. We can also pass the option *-std=c++14* with g++.

Books In Print

Advanced C++ FAQs: Volume 1 : Fundamentals

This book is not an introduction to C++. It assumes that the reader is aware of the basics of C++98 and C++03 and wants to expand her horizon to latest and greatest in the present and future of C++, including C++11 and C++1y(aka C++14). It contains selected fundamental problems with detailed solutions to all of these which will help the reader to hone her skills to solve a particular problem. The problems are marked on a scale of one(*)(simplest) to five stars(*****)(hardest).

To understand the approach better, let us look at one of the problems as follows:

*** Question 7   Generic Slide Function

Implement a generic slide function for shifting a contiguous selection of items in a sequential container like vector to a specified location either back or forth.

Solution of Question 7

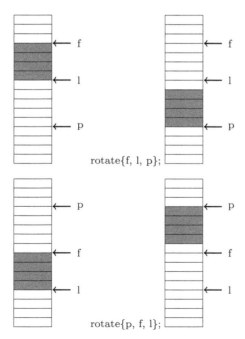

Combining these, we get:

```
1 if (p < f) rotate(p, f, l);
2 if (l < p) rotate(f, l, p);
```

Suppose we are interested in getting the final positions too, then we can write the code in C++11 as:

```
1 if (p < f) return { p, rotate(p, f, l) };
2 if (l < p) return { rotate(f, l, p), p };
```

Let us complete the code with the third case of no shifting at all:

```
1 return {f, l};
```

```
1 // I models RandomAccessIterator
2 template <typename I>
3 auto slide(I f, I l, I p) -> pair<I, I>
4 {
5     if (p < f) return { p, rotate(p, f, l) };
6     if (l < p) return { rotate(f, l, p), p };
7
8     return { f, l };
9 }
```

Forthcoming volumes will strengthen this particular approach spanning various areas of C++.

Advanced C++ FAQs: Volume 2 : Generic Programming

This book is sequel to the first volume *Advanced C++ FAQs : Volume 1 : Fundamentals*. It assumes that the reader is aware of the basics of C++98 and C++03 and wants to expand her horizon to latest and greatest in the present and future of C++, including C++11 and C++1y(aka C++14). It contains selected generic programming problems with detailed solutions to all of these which will help the reader to hone her skills to solve a particular problem. The problems are marked on a scale of one(*)(simplest) to five stars(*****)(hardest).

To understand the approach better, let us look at one of the problems as follows:

**** Question 56   metafunction : check presence of type member

Develop an utility in a form of trait-like metafunction to determine whether a type T has a type member named *type*.

Solution of Question 56

```
1 #include <type_traits>
2 #include <iomanip>
3 #include <iostream>
4
5 template< class T >
6     using void_t = void;
7     //using void_t = std::conditional_t<true, void, T>;
8
9
10 template< class, class = void >
11 struct has_type_member : std::false_type
12 { };
13
14 template< class T >
15 struct has_type_member<T, void_t<typename T::type>> : std::true_type
16 { };
17
18 struct A
```

```
19 {
20     typedef int type;
21 };
22
23 struct B
24 {
25 };
26
27 int main()
28 {
29     static_assert(has_type_member<A>::value, "");
30     static_assert(!has_type_member<B>::value, "");
31
32     std::cout << std::boolalpha;
33     std::cout << has_type_member<A>() << std::endl;
34     std::cout << has_type_member<B>() << std::endl;
35     std::cout << has_type_member< std::common_type<int, double> >{}() <<
           std::endl;
36     std::cout << has_type_member< std::common_type<int, std::string> >{}()
           << std::endl;
37
38 }
```

It prints :

```
true
false
true
false
```

Compared to traditional code that computes such a result, this version seems considerably simpler, and has no special cases (e.g., to avoid forming any pointer-to-reference type).

The purpose of the *void_t* alias template is simply to map any given type to *void*.

On some platforms, it may issue error citing unused argument T in the alias template specialization, so we may need to use the following code instead:

```
using void_t = std::conditional_t<true, void, T>;
```

conditional_t works as a workaround to ensure that our template's argument is always used.

The code features exactly two cases, each straightforward:

1. when there is a type member named *type*, the specialization is well-formed (with *void* as its second argument) and will be selected, producing a *true_type* result

2. when there is no such type member, *SFINAE* will apply, the specialization will be nonviable, and the primary template will be selected instead, yielding *false_type*.

Thus, each case obtains the appropriate result.

Kindly note that we can extend the code for *void_t* to be used for mapping a sequence of types to *void*.

```
1 template< class... >
2 struct voider { using type = void; };
3
4 template< class... T0toN >
5 using void_t = = typename voider<T0toN...>::type;
```

Forthcoming volumes will strengthen this particular approach spanning various areas of C++.

Advanced C++ FAQs: Volumes 1 & 2

This book is a combination of the following two books :

1. *Advanced C++ FAQs: Volume 1 : Fundamentals*
2. *Advanced C++ FAQs: Volume 2 : Generic Programming*

Index

www.ingramcontent.com/pod-product-compliance
Lightning Source LLC
Chambersburg PA
CBHW071006050326
40689CB00014B/3514